History of China

A Captivating Guide to Chinese History, Including Events Such as the First Emperor of China, the Mongol Conquests of Genghis Khan, the Opium Wars, and the Cultural Revolution

Free Bonus from Captivating History
(Available for a Limited time)

Hi History Lovers!

Now you have a chance to join our exclusive history list so you can get your first history ebook for free as well as discounts and a potential to get more history books for free! Simply visit the link below to join.

Captivatinghistory.com/ebook

Also, make sure to follow us on Facebook, Twitter and Youtube by searching for Captivating History.

Contents

Introduction

The history of China is complex—perhaps more complex than that of other nations. The ethnic groups that compose China go back to prehistoric times, and each group lent its own color to the enormous nation. It is not like a diluted mixture of all its cultures; rather, it is a collage.

Yet there are immutable elements still present today. Rice originated in China, and so did stir-frying. Anyone who has enjoyed a snack or two from a delightful swimming pool imitates the same practice in the water towns of China from times past. Brocade and printed silk fabrics were first created in China. Iridescent porcelain is a product of the Ming dynasty. The Chinese were among the first to develop blast furnaces. They were the first to invent fireworks and gunpowder. And the list goes on and on.

As you read this, you will note that history tends to repeat itself in the rise and fall of the many dynasties of China. However, you will also notice that there are clear distinctions between one era and the next.

In an analysis of maps showing the expansion and decline of the many dynasties throughout Chinese history, one can readily see that the smaller kingdoms frequently relocated. Some were by nomadic societies, but others were forced to do so through the fortunes or misfortunes of war. Emperors lived and died, but one can see the characteristics of their reigns as being propelled by power and expansionism, avarice, self-defense, intellectualism, altruism, wickedness, or simply by chance.

The culture of China is rich. The poetry and writing of China are permeated with feelings and are read and respected throughout the world. The Chinese have always had a reverence for their own history, which was meticulously recorded throughout the long and dusty years. Their artwork speaks with the simplicity of nature itself, and a common theme one can find is that the individual expresses himself as a part of the whole.

This idea can be found in Sinification, the spread of Chinese culture, namely the Han Chinese culture, which is a two-pronged dilemma. Practically speaking, it creates a blending of different peoples and can yield a peaceful co-existence and a semblance of harmony, but it can also condemn the richness that comes from diversity. The various cultures of Asia prize their own heritage and way of life, but Sinification tends to eliminate that. Over time, many cultures that had been Sinicized managed to find their old traditions and bring them back to the forefront. However, their lives had been inextricably changed due to Chinese involvement, and it was not always in a bad way, as the Chinese brought agricultural advancements and more forward-thinking to some cultures.

It is impossible to describe the impact China has made on all of humankind, but this book will attempt to do so by diving into its rich history.

Chapter 1 – The Land of the Yellow Emperor

The Legend of P'an Ku

From out of the chaos, the deep profoundness of the origin of life, rose Nu Kua Shih. It is said in the ancient texts that she took yellow clay in her hands and molded a man and a woman. It was up to them to keep their world healthy and whole. But they didn't always perform well, and their failure to protect the earth had ramifications.

In the world, which was composed of China, repairs were needed because of flooding. The people believed that this flooding was caused by Huang Di, the mythical "Yellow Emperor," who was displeased when his people misbehaved. The Yellow Emperor was so named because he was made of the soil, which had a distinctive yellow tinge. When the wise Nu Kua Shih saw that, she took mercy upon the people and stopped the floods. Thus, the land was saved from total destruction. China has two great rivers, the Yellow River and the Yangtze, and even to this day, flooding is a perennial problem because of the periodic flooding of those rivers.

The descendants of the first ancient people of China were farmers who dwelt in city-states. Emigration was forbidden, as their leaders realized that strength resided in numbers. Defense depended upon the population, and so did the cultivation of crops. There were peasant farmers, but there were also higher-class farmers who ran estate-like farms. Later on, the peasants worked outside walled cities, and the inner areas fostered merchants, scholars, and artisans.

The first dynasty of China was called the Xia dynasty. The foundations of the Xia lay in myths, so some scholars believe that this dynasty might not have existed at all. The establishment of the Xia dynasty is credited to a man named Yu the Great. Although Huang Di was said to have curbed the floods of the Yellow River, the Xia people believed that Nu Kua Shih was the one who actually stopped the floods, and so, they deified her.

The Xia dynasty is believed to have ruled between 2100 and 1600 BCE, if it even existed at all. The problem of its authenticity lies in the fact that are no contemporary written records of it; in fact, the earliest mention of it dates to around the 13th century BCE.

Shang and Zhou

Around 1600 BCE, the Shang dynasty came about. It had a vassal state called the Zhou. The staple food for the people of the Shang and the Zhou was rice, an ideal crop for a country that is covered in water. According to an ancient legend, rice was discovered when a dog ran through the floodwaters with mysterious seeds attached to his tail. When the people were starving, they heated the seeds in water. The seeds then expanded and became soft enough to eat. The rice saved the people, and they considered it a gift from Huang Di. The people grew rice in paddies, and they created terraces for the rice to prevent erosion. The original rice they grew was a variety of long-grain brown rice.

The upper classes enjoyed meat from cows, chickens, pigs, sheep, and deer. The lower classes and the slaves mostly lived on fish. It is interesting to note that the Chinese developed their traditional method of cutting food up into small tasty bits in ancient times. As early as the year 1000 BCE, during the Zhou dynasty, they mastered the techniques of stir-frying, steaming, and deep-frying food. It was felt that cooked food was the mark of civilization.

During the Shang dynasty, a script was developed, which consisted of a series of pictographs. In a short period of time, many of these "pictures" became less complex and more symbolic. They even had symbols to indicate phonetic pronunciation to help avoid confusion. The inscriptions spoke of births, harvests, wars, human sacrifices, and threats of war from neighboring tribes. Archeologists and linguists have isolated as many as 3,000 characters from the writings discovered from the Shang dynasty.

The great philosopher Confucius was born in 551 BCE during the Zhou era. His beliefs have inspired people for generations. The Confucian code taught obedience to proper authorities and added much to promoting a sense of self-generated integrity to the people.

Other aspects of culture of this time can be found in the various decorations they created. Most of the Shang dynasty took place during the Bronze Age, and as such, they used bronze for bowls, incense containers, ceremonial masks, wine vessels, and weapons. As the Shang dynasty faded away, so, too, did the use of bronze. Iron metallurgy wasn't fully developed until the 10th and 9th centuries BCE. As soon as that occurred, iron quickly replaced bronze for use in warfare because bronze could easily be broken in battle.

The people of the ancient Shang and Zhou dynasties mostly settled between the Yangtze and Yellow Rivers. The Yellow River was aptly named, as it does have a yellow tinge due to the sediment it picks up on its way to the sea.

The Battle of Muye

The ruler of the Zhou, King Wu, was looked upon as the chief leader of the Chinese people. In the year 1046 BCE, Di Xin, the ruler of the Shang, strongly craved the throne and even told his people that he had the Mandate of Heaven, the idea that a ruler was selected by the deities to lead the people. Natural disasters were seen as a definitive sign that a ruler had lost the Mandate of Heaven. However, when it came to war, when one side won, everyone accepted the belief that the Mandate of Heaven was on the winner's side.

According to legend, the people of the Shang were displeased with Di Xin after he married an evil woman named Daji. Di Xin, they said, became ruthless after he married her. At the Battle of Muye, located in eastern China, the warriors used pikes, spears, crossbows, and halberds. Chariots were also used, and the craftsmen designed special war chariots that were pulled by two horses and manned by two warriors.

Battles were fought in strict formation, and it was dishonorable to take advantage of an opponent's mishaps, like a broken chariot wheel. Battlefields were designated in advance, and they were placed at a distance from villages so the civilian population would be protected.

The Battle of Muye was bloody, and Di Xin had many defections from among his army, which included both soldiers and slaves. Because he lost the confidence of his people, he lost the throne, and the Shang dynasty ended with him. In the ancient narrative, the *Commentary of Zuo*, it says, "Calamity shall arise when officials lack credibility. Without supporters, one is sure to perish." After the battle, it is said that Di Xin adorned himself with jewels and set himself on fire. The Zhou then became the ruling dynasty in China, with Wu as its first king.

Societal Structure

King Wu set up a feudal structure in the country. It separated the people into classes:

      1. The king
      2. The royal household and its courtesans
      3. The sheriffs
      4. The soldiers
      5. The common people
      6. The slaves

When Wu died, his oldest son, Cheng, hadn't come of age yet (he would have been around thirteen years old_, so China was run by a regent, his uncle Duke Wen. Over the years, the various village complexes battled against one another to gain greater control. There was also an impetus to use stronger weapons, and the workers started using bog iron taken from the swamps. It was melted in furnaces and molded to create iron swords and even farming implements.

Jealousies and hegemony predominated during the Warring States period, which took place between 475 and 221 BCE. When the Zhou dynasty began to fall in the 5th century, they had to rely on armies from their allies. These states saw a chance to become the one true power of the Chinese people, and constant wars broke out between them, with alliances shifting often. Once the Jin state was broken up, three major competitors emerged—the Zhao, Wei, and Han states. Over time, though, seven states fought for the control of China: Qin, Han, Wei, Zhao, Qi, Chu, and Yan. This will be touched on a bit more in the next chapter with the rise of the Qin state and dynasty, but suffice to say, there was a lot of turmoil between the seven states.

Culture

While warriors were competing for political dominance, philosophy flourished among the people.

Confucius, who lived from 551 to 479 BCE, inspired the masses with his humanistic approach to life. He eschewed scrupulous adherence to a list of rules and regulations and instead favored a philosophy that was practical and compassionate. He was, however, very demanding in terms of respect for authority. He believed in loyalty to the state and to one's parents. The cultivation of virtue was vital to a successful life, as was unselfishness.

Taoism came into being when it was promoted by Laozi in the 4th century BCE. He taught a belief in the "Way," which is a harmonious process of living. It means that one needs to traverse the "path" of righteousness and free oneself from selfish desires. In a harmonious society, unhappiness results from wanting that which one cannot have. Unlike Confucius, Laozi didn't stress obedience but taught that one should live a life that was natural, one that coincided with the tempo of life.

The early priests were often fortune-tellers. They used small animal bones that would be thrown into a fire until they cracked. When that happened, the oracle presented his or her answer to questions their clients asked. The bones they used for divination were called "oracle bones."

The use of *Tao Te Ching*, an important text in Taoism, has a divination function and is still popular today for fortune-telling. The ancient version used sayings from Laozi. They were written in pictographs on bamboo strips. The client would ask the question, and then the strips would be thrown down, after which the fortune-teller would interpret it. Today, cards are used instead of bamboo.

Before the invention of paper, bamboo was used for writing. It was cut into strips, attached at the back, and opened out like an accordion.

Chapter 2 – Imperial China Emerges

The Qin Dynasty

As time moved on, seven states emerged as forces to be reckoned with, and each warred with the others for dominance.

Fate Foretold

The people of the states of Wei, Han, Chu, Qi, Yan, and Zhao were horrified by the ruthlessness of the Qin state that emerged in the west. The priest Bo Yangfu prophesied about the end time for the Zhou dynasty when that happened. He said, "The Zhou is coming to an end! The qi [life force] of heaven and earth is never disorderly. It is people who introduce chaos to it." And he was not wrong, for the Zhou was indeed coming to an end. In 256 BCE, the Zhou dynasty disintegrated after its defeat by the Qin state.

Qin was different from the other Warring States. They didn't follow the code of honor on the battlefield, instead striking when the opportunity was ripe. Their army was also large and well-trained, headed by competent generals who believed in the goal they were pursuing: the dominance of the Chinese states. One such general was the domineering and legalistic philosopher Shang Yang, who, in 341

BCE, successfully led the Qin army against the Wei. With that win, the two major states left to fight for dominance was Qi and Qin.

By 247, it was clear that Qin was the strongest of the lot. If the other states had united with each other, they might have been able to stand against the powerful Qin soldiers. They did not do this, and so, Qin began to swiftly conquer all seven states, starting with the Han state in 230 BCE. Next, Wei fell in 225 BCE, followed by the Chu state in 223. In 222 BCE, Zhao and Yan were conquered. Qi, knowing that its time was up, surrendered its cities without a fight. In 221 BCE, a new dynasty was born: the Qin dynasty.

Although the Qin state was able to overcome these states fairly easily, difficulties did arise. In 227 BCE, Jing Ke and Qin Wuyang of Yan planned to present King Zheng of Qin with a map of their chief city. However, within the rolled-up map was a dagger—the two were actually assassins who wanted to take the Qin state out with one swipe of a blade. However, they were not very good assassins, as Qin Wuyang was so scared that he couldn't even present the map to the king. This left the plot in Jing Ke's hands alone. As soon as the king unrolled the map, Jing Ke grabbed the dagger and attacked. The king attempted to pull his sword out but was unable to do so easily due to its length. After one of the Qin officials managed to distract Jing Ke long enough, the king drew his sword and stabbed Jing Ke nine times.

The King Zheng of this story changed his name to Qin Shi Huang when he became China's first emperor. And to ensure that the nation remained as one, the Qin sought uniformity everywhere. They introduced a detailed standardization of weights and measures. For example, carts that were pulled on the roads always left ruts after it rained, which would later harden when the mud dried. The emperor's solution was to regulate the width of axles. That way, all the ruts were in the same place, and the carts would be able to travel at an efficient speed.

The Qin was a totalitarian regime. Threatened by principles and words from the past, Qin Shi Huang burned whatever tomes and writings he could find.

The Unseen Emperor

The emperor virtually "disappeared" during his reign. He didn't want to be observed by the common people because that might make him vulnerable when he traveled, so he inaugurated a massive transportation network with a tree-lined elevated road for only himself and his entourage. It was called the Qin Direct Road, and it spanned the entire length of the states under his control.

Qin Shi Huang was also an unseen power. Signs of his changes were seen everywhere, but people weren't permitted to touch him. One of the first projects Qin Shi Huang undertook was to register the entire population. But perhaps the greatest accomplishment of the Qin dynasty was the Great Wall of China.

The Great Wall

To protect his empire from the interference of neighboring feudal lords, whose ideas might inspire disunity, the emperors had a massive wall constructed. Several walls had already been made prior, some as old as the 7th century, and Qin Shi Huang decided to have them connected in 221 BCE. As time went on, the different dynasties that ruled China repaired and added to it, creating what we know as the Great Wall today. It was maintained over the centuries to help protect the country from barbarian hordes, such as the Huns, Turks, Mongols, Khitan, Jurchens, and the Xiongnu.

The Fall of the Qin Dynasty

After the reign of Qin Shi Huang, his son, Qin Er Shi, was named the new emperor, but he was only a puppet in the hands of his eunuch, Zhao Gao. Qin was only nineteen years old, and as such, he was malleable to Zhao's domineering influence. Zhao also learned that Qin Er Shi was very gullible and created a laughing stock out of the boy by conspiring with other courtiers to convince the emperor that a horse he gave him for dinner was actually a deer.

Unfortunately, that sort of naïve behavior on the emperor's part opened up opportunities for peasant rebellions. Qin had a tendency to micromanage, and he punished people for minor infractions. Zhao made Qin become a hidden emperor, like his father, which allowed

Zhao to gain more power and blinded Qin to the gravity of the revolts that broke out during his reign. Qin Er Shi ruled for only three years. He was killed in a coup led by Zhao Gao, and the next ruler would be Ziying, who took the title of king rather than emperor.

In 207 BCE, the Qin were beaten in the Battle of Julu. After the battle, one of the rebel generals, Xiang Yu, buried 200,000 Qin soldiers alive! However, he spared the three major generals, who would go on to become kings during the Eighteen Kingdoms period. Ziying was forced to capitulate to Liu Bang, another rebel leader, thus ending the Qin Empire.

The Eighteen Kingdoms

Between 206 and 202 BCE, China became engaged in an all-out war. After the Qin Empire dissolved into eighteen various states, Xiang Yu and Liu Bang realized that China needed unification; however, they couldn't both be the supreme leader of a unified China. So, the two waged war against each other, with the other sixteen kings choosing a side.

Xiang Yu was ruthless and warlike, and he attempted to assassinate Liu. Liu, on the other hand, was a man who engendered intense loyalty among his followers. After conquering a number of states, in addition to the ones he was entitled to within the Chu state, Xiang Yu assembled a huge army and pursued Liu Bang, who controlled the Han state, with a hateful vengeance. He defeated Liu Bang after three major battles, after which Liu Bang called for an armistice.

Liu Bang initially adhered to the conditions of the agreement. However, Liu's followers knew that Xiang Yu couldn't be trusted and strongly urged their leader to break the agreement. Liu wasn't in a good position to win the war against Xiang Yu but was finally able to convince two powerful local leaders to help by bribing them with a promise of titles. It worked, and Liu Bang defeated Xiang Yu at the Battle of Galaxia in 202 BCE.

Xiang Yu was a man unaccustomed to defeat, but he stood strong with the few men he had left. However, they were soon killed, and after Xiang Yu became mortally wounded, he decided to take his own life. China was now Liu Bang's.

The Han Dynasty

Liu Bang became the emperor of the Han dynasty in 202 BCE, and he took the regnal name of Emperor Gaozu. As demonstrated throughout the period of the Eighteen Kingdoms, he was a principled man. Although he didn't like the principles of Confucius initially, he later became dedicated to the Confucian belief that moral leadership was essential to create a stable country.

As one of his first actions as emperor, Gaozu rewarded those who had helped him win. He also realized that the most important aspect of leading a country was its economy. He thus appointed Xiao He, who had helped him tremendously during the war with Xiang Yu, to be in charge of the food supplies to feed the people during times of famine. Cao Shen, another one of the men who fought on the side of the Han state, was made the chancellor, who was expected to organize and run an efficient government.

Cao Shen was a scholarly man and consulted experts in various aspects of governing. Following Confucian ideals, Cao selected leaders of the administration based on competence, honesty, and their obedience to authority, not on heredity, as it had been done in the past.

Having experienced the heavy tax burden thrust upon the people during the Qin dynasty, Cao lowered the taxes on the peasants. However, he did raise the taxes on the merchants, as they had been benefiting quite well during the wars. He nationalized the iron and salt industries when he noted that a handful of people were making an enormous fortune from it while others were being exploited.

This was called the "Golden Age of Ancient China." Gaozu created an atmosphere of creative freedom so that the country would be successful, and the economy was stimulated by Gaozu's efforts to open the Silk Road routes, which connected the East to the West, to facilitate trade. Because of the desirability of silk, one of the most important inventions was that of a primitive loom, which gave Chinese craftsmen the ability to produce patterned clothing to sell via the Silk Road. Archeologists have discovered models of that loom in Laojunshan in Shu province that date back to the Han dynasty.

The Han-Xiongnu War, 133 BCE–89 CE

In 133 BCE, Emperor Wu of the Han dynasty attacked the nomadic and fierce Xiongnu. The Xiongnu were very aggressive and skilled horsemen, originating in the steppe regions north of today's China. The Xiongnu made enemies of many nearby tribes by raiding their farms, destroying their granaries, and confiscating their lands. Emperor Wu created an alliance between his people and the Yuezhi people, who were also nomadic, as well as excellent warriors and horsemen. Some of Wu's warriors were infantrymen and had to fight on foot.

Around the year 114 BCE, the Silk Road, a network of trade routes that connected the East and the West, was expanded by the Han dynasty. Wu used the Silk Road to transport his forces to fight the Xiongnu. He was assisted by General Huo Qubing, who led the cavalry forces. By the year 110, they had forced the Xiongnu to retreat into the Gobi Desert.

Chapter 3 – The Supremacy of the Han, 202 BCE–220 CE

In 53 BCE, the Xiongnu Empire was in turmoil. Huhanye had rebelled in 59 BCE with the hopes of becoming the ruler, but his brother, Zhizhi, still stood in the way. Zhizhi was stronger than Huhanye, who decided to go to the Han for help. In order to gain their assistance, Huhanye made peace with the Han, and Xiongnu became a tributary state. In those days, it was customary to send someone of royal blood as a hostage to the dominant power. Along with a caravan of gifts, precious cloth, and jewels, Huhanye sent his son, Shuloujutang, to live at the Han court. In response, the Han sent a bronze plaque that read, "To Han obedient, friendly and loyal chief of Xiongnu of Han." It was to be displayed prominently and served as a pledge of loyalty to the Han emperor.

Zhizhi also sent his son to the Han in 53 BCE, and while he sent envoys in the following years with tribute, he failed to come in person to present them, as was expected. This was considered to be a great insult, and since his brother, Huhanye, had respectfully followed protocol, the Han backed him. In 36 BCE, the Han surrounded Zhizhi's fortress and proceeded to kill over 1,000 of the Xiongnu, along with Zhizhi and his wives. The victorious Han general, Chen Tang, took the severed head of Zhizhi to Emperor Yuan of Han.

Beginning of the Strife

The Han dynasty, too, was besieged with jealousies, internal conflicts, and revolts. This cost the empire money, and the imperial treasury was slowly depleted to keep pace with the cost of these wars.

In the year 9 CE, Wang Mang usurped the throne. He had no royal blood in him, but he still declared to the people that he and he alone had the Mandate of Heaven. Some historians view his grab for power as just that, while others believe he had great plans for social reforms. While Wang Mang believed his rule to be separate from the Han dynasty, naming it the Xin dynasty, most historians consider it to be an interregnum period, as the Xin dynasty ended with Wang Mang's death.

The unrest only grew under Wang Mang's rule, triggering uprisings and wars, especially in the lands of the Eastern Han. While Wang Mang's reforms were progressive at the beginning of his rule, which included the abolition of slavery, they didn't please the people, and he ended up reverting back to the old ways. His plans for the economy didn't pan out well either, and by 17 CE, the imperial coffers were empty, which wasn't helped by the rampant corruption taking place. As the taxes increased and the corruption in government remained, the belligerent peasants united and rebelled. Wang fought against them but lost more and more support. After that, the populace surrendered to the authority of the rightful Han heir, Liu Xiu, who became Emperor Guangwu.

The Good Emperor Guangwu

Emperor Guangwu faced many pretenders when he ascended the throne in 25 CE. For instance, Gongsun Shu formed the Cheng dynasty the same year, which grew to cover a large area of China. Guangwu was a man of peace and detested the bloodshed of Han against Han, but there was no other option but to fight the Cheng.

However, the Cheng dynasty was not the only threat that Guangwu had to defeat in order to unify the empire. Several regional powers popped up, and Guangwu spent many years in defeating them. Guangwu preferred the diplomatic approach, which worked in some cases. Wei Xiao of the Xizhou and Dou Rong of Liang province submitted to the emperor. Guangwu appointed Dou Rong as the prime comptroller of his region. Guangwu often awarded titles and honors to the warlords who submitted but never sufficient enough power to overtake the empire.

Not all so easily acquiesced to the Han. Liu Yong, who claimed to be the actual Han emperor and controlled the Jiangsu area (current-day Henan province), attacked the Han. In 29 CE, he and his son were killed by Emperor Guangwu's forces. By the year 30 CE, the Han had united all of eastern China.

However, Emperor Guangwu still had Gongsun Shu and the powerful Cheng dynasty to deal with. In 33, Guangwu was able to place all of his attention on Gongsun. After several battles, Guangwu had his warriors surround Gongsun in his capital in 36. Gongsun was tricked into believing that Guangwu's soldiers were weaker than they appeared, and in the battle that followed, he was mortally wounded. His entire family was massacred, as were members of other prominent officials of the Cheng dynasty. Once the Cheng dynasty fell, all of China was united once again.

Contributions of the Han

The Chinese people were gifted mathematicians, and the Han invented the system of Gaussian Elimination, which is a process in linear algebra used to eliminate all but one variable in an equation. Gaussian Elimination would permit a numeric solution in determining measurements and quantities. It was part of the *Nine Chapters on the Mathematical Art* and predated mathematics in Europe.

In the year 105 CE, Cai Lun perfected the invention of paper. It was made from hemp, tree bark, and rags and fabrics that were formed by splitting up old fishing nets. In the year 132, Zhang Heng invented the first seismometer, a device that measures earthquakes. He was also a gifted astronomer and astonished the scientific community by saying that the moon doesn't shine with its own light but rather the reflected light of the sun. Zhang Heng was also the first to create an accurate map of the stars in the celestial hemisphere.

The Han developed many other things that we take for granted today. The wheelbarrow, the magnetic compass, the loom, and the hot air balloon were all invented by the great minds of the Han dynasty. The earliest versions of the blast furnace and the steering wheels of ships can also be contributed to Chinese civilization.

The Yellow Turban Rebellion, 184–205

Taoist traditions were constantly practiced throughout these trying times. Many holy priests, magicians, and practitioners of early Chinese herbal medicine helped the less fortunate, sick, and vulnerable. The founder of the Yellow Turbans, Zhang Jue, was a devotee of Taoism. He announced to the people that the Han domination was coming to an end. He stated that a new time awaited and pronounced, "The Azure Sky is already dead; the Yellow Sky will soon rise. When the year is jiazi [184 CE], there will be prosperity under Heaven!" The "Azure Sky" refers to the Han dynasty.

According to the legends, people reported that they saw the sacred signs, which included a plume of black smoke in the imperial audience chamber that was in the shape of a dragon and an earthquake, which occurred in a distant province. Due to the earthquake, which people claimed occurred in 184 CE, a fissure broke the earth open, and warriors emerged. The warriors wore yellow turbans to proclaim their fellowship.

However, the real truth is not so much in the realm of the supernatural. Zhang Jue and his brothers, Zhang Bao and Zhang Liang, were faith healers. They taught the art of Chinese herbal medicine to their pupils. The religious aspect of these leaders seemed to serve as a justification for the violence that accompanied this revolt.

Sima Qian, a Chinese historian and a contemporary under the Han regime, wrote that many military feats were attributed to the Zhang brothers. In one transcript written by Sima Qian, it said that Zhang Bao "spread his hair and held out his sword, summoning spirits with magic arts. Suddenly a tempest sprung up, and the air became a black mist." From that mist, the tale goes on to say that the numerous troops emerged from the mist and went into battle.

The Yellow Turban Rebellion was widespread, and they even recruited non-Chinese to participate in it. Some joined to bring down the Han Empire, but many who joined were warlords seeking to expand their own petty little kingdoms.

There were many factions that split off from the initial membership of the Yellow Turbans, who battled for control of various provinces. Little by little, the factions were suppressed. When the infamous warrior Cao Cao waged against the Yellow Turbans in Yu province in 205, it finally fizzled out. After this was accomplished, Cao Cao had successfully united northern China and then proceeded to the south.

The Battle of Red Cliffs, 208

The northern warlord Cao Cao decided to conquer the lands south of the Yangtze River: Zhouzhuang, Wuzhen (Wuhan), Xitang, and Tangli. They were ancient water towns, networked with canals. Today, many tourists and residents can travel by boat and dine at the seaside stands, enjoying some of the culinary delicacies the vendors create. Today's great city and seaport of Shanghai is also within this area.

Cao Cao invaded those picturesque and important cities in 208. Although he was a formidable warlord, he made a mistake that other invaders often make—he didn't familiarize himself with the environmental characteristics of the area. The Yangtze, like the Yellow River, overflowed several times during the seasons, and Cao Cao didn't know this. So, even though he and his troops outnumbered the home forces, his horses, his warriors, and their weapons became stuck in the muck and mud of the water towns. Cao Cao's soldiers were forced to wade through the swamps and were sometimes victimized when they reached patches of quicksand. In fact, Liu Bei, one of the leaders of the defenders of the water towns, laughed and said to Cao Cao's warriors, "After passing through hell, like quicksand, not even a blade of grass has grown. You will definitely die here!"

Some historians have called the Battle of Red Cliffs a naval battle, and, in a way, it was. When the enemy in the south launched fire ships across the Yangtze, those who hadn't got stuck in the mud leaped into what water they could find. Cao Cao was then forced to retreat.

Through the centuries, the figure of Cao Cao carries with him a legacy of power that attracts the egotistical of any age. Of him, it was said, "You're wise enough to rule the world and perverse enough to destroy the world."

The Three Kingdoms, 220–280

Cao Cao's son, Cao Pi, created his own state called Wei in 220. When Emperor Xian of the Han abdicated, Cao Pi took the throne, ending the Han dynasty once and for all. Soon after this, two rivals, Liu Bei and Sun Quan, created the Shu Han and Wu states, respectively.

Wei, Shu, and Wu created the foundation for today's most popular video games. These games are historically based and feature the figures that are highlighted in this book. Cao Pi, for instance, is the questionable hero of the evil, dark worlds that permeated the Han Chinese in these turbulent times.

The emperors of the three kingdoms were young and inexperienced, so their courtiers, who were castrated eunuchs, manipulated the country and gained power. Those were dark days, but homegrown leaders rose from among the people. These leaders rose up and, according to an ancient storyteller, announced, "We vow to stand by each other and be blood brothers forever. Let us agree to protect the people of our homeland!" This tale was written in the *Romance of the Three Kingdoms* by Luo Guanzhong. It is a story about the warlords of legend and lore loosely based on the history of this chaotic period. It is a tale about subterfuge and treason and talks of courage against cowardice.

The three kingdoms were eventually unified in 280, with Sima Yan conquering the last-standing kingdom of Wu. Sima Yan then established the Jin dynasty and was known to posterity as Emperor Wu.

The Jin Dynasty, 266–420

Although the Jin dynasty united the areas of what now is eastern China, the government split the districts up into a complex system of smaller administrations. As many as eleven existed in the year 400, but it eventually increased to sixteen. Territorial expansions occurred, and the original Jin state was then divided into regions to the north and northwest—South Yan, North Yan, Wei (named after the original Wei state), Xia, and Liao.

While the officials busied themselves with administrative affairs, the artisans of the area developed fine porcelain pottery called celadon, also known as greenware. The artifacts were finely hewn and are quite valuable today. Greenware was the precursor of the fine tri-colored glazes created during the following Tang dynasty.

Murder and Assassinations

Cruelty spawned from the jealousies and the evil-doings of the last ruler of the Jin dynasty, which ultimately led to its demise. Emperor An was the legitimate heir when he came to the throne in 397, but he was developmentally disabled. Because of his disability, he was strangled in 419 at the age of 37 by order of his own regent, Liu Yu. Liu Yu was one of the many regents that Emperor An had, as it was a highly coveted position. Liu Yu then proclaimed the boy's brother, Sima Dewen, to be the new emperor. However, Emperor Gong (Sima Dewen's regnal name) yielded to Liu Yu's power a year later, surrendering the throne to him. Liu Yu was concerned that Sima would eventually regain the position, so he decided to take matters in his own hands and had the 35-year-old Sima asphyxiated with a blanket. With the death of Sima Dewen, the Jin dynasty met its end.

The Northern and Southern Dynasties, 386–589

The evil that had been kindled during the Jin dynasty spread throughout the country, giving rise to many divisions and sub-divisions in order to satisfy the petty rulers of the smaller provinces.

Power was divided between the northern and southern kingdoms, with the kingdoms falling and rising to new kingdoms as time went by. At times, kingdoms existed simultaneously with another, such as the northern kingdoms of Western Wei (535–557) and the Northern Qi (550–577).

Since the Northern and Southern dynasties lasted for a little over 200 years, many rulers rose up, and this book will examine one such ruler. In 561, Emperor Wu of Northern Zhou came to power. In the early part of his reign, he let his cousin, Yuwen Hu, do much of the ruling, as Yuwen Hu was essentially the man who placed Emperor Wu on the throne. Over time, though, the emperor amassed more personal power, and he successfully attacked Yuwen Hu in 572. The rest of his reign was spent on the idea of uniting China under one ruler, but Emperor Wu suddenly died in 578, leaving the throne to his son, Yuwen Yun.

Sadly, Yuwen Yun, who became known as Emperor Xuan upon ascending the throne, was a poor leader. His father's attempts at unifying China were thrown out the window, as Emperor Xuan sought to return to traditionalist values instead of attending to more important matters. Less than a year after assuming the throne, Xuan passed it onto his son, Emperor Jing. In 580, after the death of Emperor Xuan, Emperor Jing's father-in-law, Yang Jian took power and established his own dynasty, the Sui dynasty, in 581. His royal name was Emperor Wen.

Throughout the time of the Northern and Southern dynasties, people sought refuge in Buddhism, Taoism, and Confucianism. Although Buddhism was introduced much later than the other two religions, it quickly rose in popularity. While these three religions vied for dominance, the holy priests still recognized the importance of all three belief systems. In the 6th century, the people erected glorious temples for worship within the Hanging Monastery, an elegant structure carved into the cliffs in northeast China. According to legend, it was designed by a monk named Liaoran, and it contains exquisite carvings, pillared balconies, multiple staircases, and painted statues of Buddhist priests and worshippers. The marvelous structure is a tourist site today.

The Sui Dynasty, 581–618

Although the Sui dynasty didn't last for very long, Emperor Wen was able to unite all of China under one rule. Besides this great accomplishment, the Sui Dynasty also constructed the Grand Canal. Until that time, soldiers on long campaigns had to stop to grow their own vegetables and grain for food. Once food could be sent to them by boat, it was far more convenient and less time-consuming.

The Grand Canal was and still is the longest canal in the world. It is 1,776 miles long, and it starts in Beijing and runs northwest to Hangzhou. The Grand Canal connects the Yellow River with the Yangtze, as well as four other minor rivers. After the canal was built, trading flourished among the provinces. Trade was vital to the empire because its ships carried grain to the imperial court and to the eastern coast.

Emperor Wen of the Sui knew that the area under his control was frequently being flooded by the Yellow and Yangtze Rivers. So, in 584, he hired engineer Yuwen Kai to alleviate the problem. Yuwen Kai and his engineers created smaller canals to divert the water. They built the Guangtong Canal to stem off the overflow from the Grand Canal, and they also dug the Shanyang Canal to allow for increased traffic between the Yangtze and Huai Rivers. Many scientific studies are currently being conducted on the Grand Canal regarding its environmental impact, and the most promising results are being implemented.

In 594, there was a severe drought. To cut back on food, the emperor and his court abstained from meat for a year. When Yang Guang, Wen's son and future heir, asked that his father to establish an elaborate festival to the gods to relieve the drought, Wen did so. However, Wen was extremely frugal, and he didn't give much money toward the festival.

In the spring of 604, the emperor made preparations to move to Renshou Palace, where he customarily spent the summers after it was built in 593. A sorcerer, however, warned him that if he went there, he would not return. Ignoring that warning, Wen went to Renshou anyway and died there from an illness. He was revered for generations to come.

His son, Yang Guang, assumed the throne, taking the regnal name Emperor Yang. According to interpretations of an ancient plaque designed between 604 and 617, scholars indicate that Yang was hedonistic and overworked his laborers, who were recruited to make his life pleasurable. History seems to bear that out because peasant rebellions were frequent during his rule. In addition, Yang made the futile attempt to conquer Korea and parts of what is Vietnam today.

One of his generals and governors, Li Yuan, began to amass personal power. In 617, Li managed to capture the capital and placed Yang's grandson on the throne. Once Emperor Yang died in 618, Li removed the young emperor and declared himself to be the new ruler of China. He created one of the most influential Chinese dynasties: the Tang dynasty.

Chapter 4 – The Golden Age: The Tang Dynasty, 618–907

In 618, Li Yuan took the royal name Emperor Gaozu. He adopted many of the wise practices of Emperor Wen. Adult males were granted lots of land on which they paid taxes. Gaozu also established a monetary system using copper coins and wrote a code of law. Unfortunately, he met the same fate as former Emperor Yang of the Sui dynasty. In 626, one of his three sons, Li Shimin, killed his brothers. His father, afraid of what his son's next actions might be, abdicated and left the throne to him. Shimin was then known as Emperor Taizong. Despite his criminal ways, he was an effective emperor. Life as a royal was, at best, extremely risky for siblings and close relatives. As such, these were not the kindest of times.

In 657, Taizong annexed the Eastern Turkic Khaganate and expanded the empire. The Turkic Khaganate, located in current-day Kyrgyzstan, was good for growing pomegranates, grapes, and rice. In addition, the Turks in that region were rather compliant and adjusted well to their tributary status.

Taizong did much good for his country by creating storage granaries in case of famine, and he also inaugurated a civil examination to ascertain administrative ability for those who served in governmental offices. The Tang dynasty expanded its sphere of influence into the Persian Empire in Central Asia and today's Afghanistan.

The "Wicked" Empress

Taizong died in 649. His son, Gaozong was the next in line. However, Gaozong was in love with one of his father's concubines, Wu Zetian. Wu was very anxious to gain control of the matters of the state.

In 660, her wish came true when Gaozong began to suffer from an illness, allowing Wu to seize the opportunity to gain a lot of power. She was essentially able to rule in his stead, but to do so safely, she needed to eliminate her competition. She found excuses to put Gaozong's other wives under house arrest, and she didn't just target these influential women. In 652, Wu gave birth to a son, Li Hong. Four years later, he became the crown prince, and as time went by, he became more assertive and outspoken against his mother's actions. According to contemporary historians, she poisoned him in 675. Considering the things she did to keep power, it is entirely possible that she was the one behind his death.

In 683, Emperor Gaozong died and was succeeded by Wu's other son, Li Zhe, who became Emperor Zhongzong. All was well until Zhongzong tried to appoint his father-in-law, Wei Xuanzhen, as chancellor. Wu swiftly fired him and exiled her son. Obviously, Wu did not hide her ambitions or power. She then placed her youngest son, Li Dan (Emperor Ruizong), on the throne.

Although she still held all of the power, with her son ruling as a figurehead, she wanted more. In 690, Wu announced a new dynasty, the Zhou dynasty, and attempted to rule it herself. To bolster her authority, she wrote the *Great Cloud Sutra*, which foretold a female emperor would be responsible for eradicating problems such as famine, worry, and illness from the world. She also claimed to be an incarnation of Maitreya, the successor to Buddha.

To this day, Wu Zetian has been the only female emperor of China. Although it was novel for a woman to rule, she honestly was not much different from other male emperors. She introduced some new reforms, but she overall kept things the way they had been, bringing about a period of stability to the nation. However, the people did not recognize her proclaimed new dynasty and did not care for her methods of gaining power (some of which were most likely exaggerated—this book only skims the surface of what she was accused of doing). In 705, a large palace coup took place. Wu Zetian was forced to surrender her position, and Zhongzong was restored as emperor. Unfortunately for Zhongzong, he made the fatal error of marrying someone much like his mother.

In 710, Zhongzong died. Most historians agree that he was murdered by his scheming wife, Empress Wei, who craved a life similar to Wu Zetian's. Conspiracies and counter-conspiracies overtook the court, as the various courtesans and court officials attempted to gain more power in the empire. To frighten Wei, the conspirators murdered her two nephews and cousin. Wei then fled to a camp of palace guards. However, they were also disgusted by her nefarious behavior, and Wei was beheaded! Her body and those of her associates were displayed in public on the streets of Chang'an.

In 710, Zhongzong's brother, Ruizong, ascended to the throne once more. However, after hearing some dire predictions from his astrologers, he retired and passed the throne to his son, Emperor Xuanzong, in 712. Xuanzong was a wise man who surrounded himself with capable chancellors. He steeped himself in Chinese philosophy and paved the way for prosperity and peace in the realm.

The Cultural Achievements of the Tang

The Tang dynasty is noted in the world of art and literature for its treasures. Many of these works of art were transported on the Grand Canal and the Silk Road to be sold to other countries.

Yi Xing was an engineer who developed uses for hydraulic power, which farmers incorporated into devices similar to the waterwheel to use on their farms. Yi adopted that same movement to create a celestial globe with toothed gears to measure the planets' movements. In 725, he invented a kind of clock that operated on the movement of water into different-sized scoops, which were divided into measurements that marked the hours and days in a five-day cycle. It was equipped with bells and drums to ring the hour and quarter-hours.

Li Bai was one of the most noteworthy poets during the Tang dynasty. His works reflect nature and are filled with compassionate, deep, and thoughtful reflections. However, he used simple words. The Taoist nature of his work is clear: "We sit together, the mountain and me, until only the mountain remains." Between 779 and 831, another fine writer, Yuan Zhen, wrote the *Yingying's Biography*, which was later used in Chinese operas. Contemporary histories also wrote during this period, providing future scholars with a wealth of material on the politics, practices, and culture of the Tang.

Woodblock printing was one of the Tang's most notable accomplishments, as it was a way that the Chinese could print their sacred histories, stories, and poetry. Not only that, but the technique was applied to fabrics as well. This helped seamstresses create beautiful patterns on their clothing.

Printing was a rather tedious process, as it required many wooden blocks to be carved. The pictographs that formed Chinese characters also had to be cut in relief. Letters, of course, needed to be printed as if in a mirror image in order to be read. Then the layout of the words was pressed on silk. The Chinese are very artistic and used many motifs to decorate their fabrics. Flowers and plants were the most common themes. They liked bright colors, so a technique of reproducing color was invented. Crushed berries or minerals were mixed with water to produce the colors. In cases where more than one color was needed, a picture was separated into colors, and multiple woodblocks would be used. Prior to the computer, artists utilized color separation to create a cohesive and attractive design.

Sancai is a form of earthenware pottery characteristic of the Tang period. Tri-color vases and figures, mostly used in Tang tombs, were very popular. The Taoists of Tang believed in an afterlife and likewise believed that a person's tomb should include all the items necessary in life. Statues of hunters, servants, and horses were found inside many of these tombs.

Sancai was composed of bauxite, a valuable resource even today. Today, China is the world's second-largest producer of bauxite. It is used for making abrasives, cement products, and aluminum. For the Tang pottery and ceramics, the bauxite figure needed two firings in the kiln in order to create a tri-color statuette. Predominant colors found in Tang China were brown, green, and red. Since bauxite is very versatile, glazes could be made from it as well. The application of these glazes added to the unusual beauty of the works.

The Tang also oversaw the expansion of the Longmen Grottoes. They had been carefully carved into the side of a mountain. In the mountain, which supports the grottoes, there are over 2,000 caves with figures, nearly 2,500 stelae, and 100,000 statues. Empress Wu, despite her failings, had an appreciation of art and respect for Buddhism, so she contributed to its upkeep.

Metalwork was also produced by the gifted artisans of the period. They used precious metals, such as silver and gold. Bronze was also used to make mirrors and cups.

Perhaps one of the lesser-known inventions of the Chinese is something called sticky rice mortar. It was first used around 500 CE, which was before the time of the Tang dynasty, but it became widely used during the Tang. So, in essence, waterproofing was made possible due to the use of rice! When sticky rice soup was mixed with flaked, heated, and moistened lime from limestone, it created a mortar suitable for bricklaying and patching up gaps in houses. It was even used to repair holes in the Great Wall.

Gunpowder!

The Chinese alchemists were well known as healers and magicians. They spent many hours experimenting with elements found from rocks and plants. When sulfur, charcoal, and saltpeter are combined and heated, the mixture explodes. No doubt this was discovered by accident when the substance was placed in a closed container with one end open. Chinese alchemists were well known as a risk-taking group of people, with their singed beards, missing eyebrows, and burns on their faces from the many different chemicals they mixed together. After many attempts, they were able to achieve proto-fireworks. They were used at festivals as primitive firecrackers or simply to impress a crowd of admirers. It wasn't until the 10th century that gunpowder was used in warfare. The Chinese were the first to invent the substance, and it wouldn't spread throughout Eurasia until the 13th century.

In 858, a Taoist text printed a recipe for it as six parts sulfur, one-part birthwort root, and six parts saltpeter. "Birthwort root" is a related genus to the beautiful clematis plant. The rhizomes (horizontal roots) of the plant were used in this formula, but they aren't necessary to create the mixture that makes gunpowder.

The Chinese text that delineated the chemical recipe for gunpowder went on to warn the readers that the resulting product could cause burns on one's skin and could even burn down houses if mixed inside one's laboratory. The early version of gunpowder was called *huo yao*, meaning "fire medicine."

Government

The administration of the Tang had three departments that were tasked with the job of issuing and reviewing policies and seeing to it that the people were aware of the latest pronouncements. Six ministries handled a wide assortment of duties, including finances, military, and justice. Many of the emperors had careful tallies made of the populations in their various provinces and tributary states so that proper taxes could be collected and tax regulations enforced. The Tang also had a postal service with routes that were about 20,000 miles long altogether.

The An Lushan Rebellion

To mar an otherwise peaceful time, a disgruntled general named An Lushan persuaded his warriors to rebel in 755. He declared himself to be the emperor of northern China, and the new Yan dynasty was formed, which existed at the same time as the Tang dynasty. An Lushan's first move was to capture Luoyang, which became his capital. The forces then planned to move on the Chinese capital of Chang'an (today's Xian). It took some time to capture it, but by 756, it belonged to An Lushan and his forces.

The Seven-Year Yan Dynasty

Emperor Xuanzong of the Tang hired as many as 22,000 mercenaries, some of whom were from the northwestern area of China. Many of them were Uyghurs, who were reportedly Muslims of Turkish origin. Originally, they lived in the Tarim Basin (north-central China) but had been supplanted throughout the centuries. Currently, they reside in diaspora communities in Kazakhstan, **Kyrgyzstan**, Uzbekistan, and throughout Europe and the Americas.

During the An Lushan Rebellion, there were murders and conspiracies among the rebel generals, who craved lucrative positions in the new Yan dynasty. In fact, An Lushan was murdered by his own son, An Qingxu, after he became enraged by his father's threats directed at his friends. One of the powerful generals, Shi Siming, then killed An Qingxu. Shi Siming's son, Shi Chaoyi, killed his father and proclaimed himself Emperor Suzong. This all took place within four years, between 757 and 761. As a result, a number of the generals became incensed by this internecine turmoil and abandoned the Yan cause. By 763, the cause was lost, and Shi Chaoyi committed suicide to avoid capture.

The Ebbing of the Tang Dynasty

The An Lushan Rebellion was not the cause of the fall of the Tang. Under Emperor Xuanzong's guidance, art, literature, and learning permeated the land. However, toward the end of his reign, Xuanzong took an even greater interest in his concubines, especially his favorite, Yang Guifei. He paid less attention to ruling, leaving it in the hands of his advisors.

Emperor Xuanzong gave Yang Guifei anything she wanted, whether it was gowns, jewels, or elaborate parties. However, she then started asking the emperor to appoint her family members to important positions in the administration. He passed that duty to one of his chancellors, Li Linfu, with instructions to do so. Li Linfu assigned the Yang family to lucrative governmental posts, and he even put some of his own personal friends in these positions as well. As a result, the civil service system of administering tests to prospective administrators was neglected. Hence, many vital positions were held by virtual incompetents. In addition, many of these officials weren't even Chinese. They were foreign nationals who had other interests closer to heart than China.

The emperor's closest friends told him that Yang and her family were harmful to the empire. He reluctantly gave his assent for her to be taken care of. In 756, the year after the An Lushan Rebellion had started, she was strangled, and her body was buried in a simple manner. The emperor felt much remorse, although he knew that such matters were often handled violently. Emperor Xuanzong was also saddened by her nearly anonymous burial and sent his eunuchs to rebury her properly in 757. Unfortunately, Yang's body had decomposed, but the eunuchs found a bag of fragrances and dried flower petals in her coffin and brought it to him. Upon seeing it, he wept uncontrollably and was consumed with guilt and loss.

In 806, the Taoist poet Bai Juyi wrote the *Song of Everlasting Regret* about Xuanzong's tragic experience. One stanza reads: "On one night in Longevity Hall, let's be two birds flying side by side. Let's be two branches on the earth inseparably tied. The sky and the earth will not be eternal, however. Only this regret remains and lasts forever and ever."

By 757, Xuanzong was no longer emperor. When he fled from the An Lushan Rebellion in 756, his son, Li Heng, had taken the throne. The rule of Emperor Suzong (Li Heng) was marked by internal power struggles and the An Lushan Rebellion. After the death of Suzong in 762, Emperor Daizong took the throne. While the rebellion was put down during his reign, other rebellions broke out from various warlords, and they essentially ruled as separate states, barely pledging any sort of loyalty to the emperor. The succeeding emperors were unable to unite China effectively, which eventually led to the disintegration of the Tang dynasty.

Back to the Beginning

The Tang had risen at a time when warlords ruled kingdoms and spent their regimes either gratifying themselves or defending their mini-kingdoms. And it was clear that history was repeating itself once again. The last Tang emperor, Ai, was only fourteen years old when he was forced off the throne. With that move, the Tang dynasty died—not with the blast of gunpowder nor with the blow of a sword but with the plaintive sigh of a boy. The year was 907.

Chapter 5 – The Song Dynasty, 960–1279

Following the Tang Dynasty, there was a period of continuing chaos in the leadership of China and its administration. After 907, when the Tang dynasty collapsed, the chaos existed for 53 more years. The period known as the Five Dynasties and Ten Kingdoms took place between 907 and 960. Eight land segments in the southeast were occupied by the Wu, Min, Shu, the later Zhou, Liang (or Liao), Wuyue, the northern Han, and the southern Han, Jingnan and Annam states. The larger portions of China were settled by the Khitans (Mongols), the North Jan, the Shatuo (a Sinicized Turkic tribe), the state of Da Chang Hi, Tufan (Tibetans), and the Uyghurs.

A Prophecy Initiates the Song Dynasty

The emperor-to-be of the Song dynasty was foretold by an unknown prophet who told military leaders and chancellors that Zhao Kuangyin had received the Mandate of Heaven, meaning that he had the approval of the deities to rule as emperor. He actually became emperor during a coup, although the prophecy most likely helped to launch him on the throne. He was then known as Emperor Taizu. He wanted to unite all of the small kingdoms into one large one. He began his rule in 960, but his dream would not come true during his reign, although he did manage to unify a good chunk of China.

During the first year of his reign, he reduced threats to his unity plan by awarding the high-ranking military commanders with a grand buffet, as well as generous estates and money for retirement. After some negotiations, the plan worked. Taizu initiated his plan of uniting the kingdoms, and a period of peace followed. After that, the Song territory expanded.

The "Shadows by the Candle and Sounds from an Axe"

One night, when he was 49 years old, Taizu was ill and retired to his chamber. No one was permitted to enter, as he was sleeping. However, in the middle of a dark night, observers reported that they looked up into the window of the emperor's chamber and saw the light of a candle dancing on the wall. Then they saw a tall black shadow leaning over the emperor's bed. The next thing they heard was the sound of an ax falling on the wooden floor and then nothing more.

In the morning, the emperor was found dead. No concrete evidence has arisen to confirm this story, but it has remained popular nonetheless. It is certainly suspicious that his younger brother, Zhao Kuangyi (Emperor Taizong), took the throne in 976 instead of Taizu's sons.

Taizong conquered the lands of the Northern Han and Wuyue. Although he attempted to conquer the Liao lands, he didn't succeed, having lost miserably at the Battle of the Gaoliang River in 979. Taizong's forces also ventured outside his territory to try to capture Dai Viet (today's Vietnam). That, too, was unsuccessful. However, it led to the introduction of Champa rice, which had been grown only in Dai Viet. It is a rice hybrid that matures faster and can be harvested twice in one season.

Taizong's successor, Emperor Zhenzong, was irritated by the failure of the Chinese to conquer the Liao dynasty of the Khitans back in 979. He felt he could conquer them and attempted to do so in the year 1004. The Song lost, and as a consequence, the emperor became subservient to them. This entailed the paying of annual tributes. On several occasions, Zhenzong added Champa rice to his tributes, and that served to mellow the disposition of the Khitan people.

Emperor Renzong succeeded Zhenzong in 1022. Although he was admired by the Chinese as being fair-minded and tolerant, the emperor was an incurable pacifist. In a questionable effort to prevent the Western Xia state in the west from attacking, Renzong paid hefty bribes to their enemy, the Liao state, so as to maintain a balance of power. While it wasn't an unwise decision considering the odds, it did create a hole in the country's treasury. Renzong reigned until 1063. Not unexpectedly, the head of the Liao dynasty paid his respects at Renzong's funeral.

The Artist Emperor

The earlier Song emperors focused upon the expansion of the Song dynasty. However, Emperor Huizong, who ruled from 1100 to 1126, was in a different category. His contribution wasn't one of military might or conquest; it was to the preservation and prolongation of Chinese culture and art. Huizong was a master calligrapher and rendered beautiful and delicate silk paintings of birds and flowers. His calligraphy style, called "Slender Gold," opened up a whole new way of artistic expression for other artists and calligraphers. He also wrote elegant poetry.

Huizong knew his limitations and admitted that he was not a man of might. He neglected the military, and when the Jurchen nomads of the Jin dynasty from the north invaded Liao, Huizong allied with them. This got rid of the Liao state, but it also meant that the Jurchen had no other enemy in the area but the Song. Huizong wanted to flee, but his advisors begged him to abdicate first. His son, Emperor Qinzong, became the ruler of a tumultuous period.

Sadly, Emperor Qinzong was not a strong military leader either. Although the Jurchens gave up the siege of Bianjing in 1126, the Song capital, the Song was forced to sign a treaty, agreeing to send the Jin dynasty tributes every year. The treaty only placated the Jurchens for so long, and they came back in 1127 and finally entered the capital.

Huizong was sent to a distant region for the last eight years of his life, where he was forever isolated from the people he loved. Tragically, he died there in poverty.

In 1127, the Song dynasty retreated south of the Yangtze River. This is why historians break the Song dynasty into two parts: the Northern Song and the Southern Song.

In 1206, the Song again went to war against the Jin, who ruled the north, under the urging of Chancellor Han Tuozhou. Emperor Ningzong felt that the Jin had been weakened by a string of natural disasters, so he took advantage. It didn't work, though, and the Song lost their bid to regain their northern lands. A peace treaty was signed in 1208, and to make matters worse, the Song government was forced to reinstate their tribute payments.

The Mongols' Attack against the Jin Dynasty

In 1211, the great Genghis Khan of the Mongols attacked the Northern Song region, which was held by the Jin. The Mongols were able to make the Jin into a vassal state. However, the Jin made some moves that the Mongols did not like; namely, they moved the capital from Beijing to Kaifeng. The Mongols retaliated and conquered the Jin dynasty entirely in 1234.

The Song had been allied with the Mongols during this, but when they stepped out of bounds and took over some important cities, such as Kaifeng and Chang'an, the Mongols reacted with force. In 1259, the Mongols moved in to invade the Song, and they did so in the typical Mongol style, with brute force and swift maneuvers.

While the Song won some battles, mainly due to the sudden death of Ogedei Khan, Genghis Khan's son, who took over after his father had died, the Mongols often had the upper hand. One of the most important battles, the Battle of Xiangyang, took place between 1267 and 1273. Kublai Khan, Genghis Khan's grandson, who was now the leader of the Mongol Empire, and his brother, Hulagu Khan, partook in this battle. Kublai and Hulagu both had an interest in the town of Xiangyang because it was near the great trading center in Hangzhou just to the west. Xiangyang had an impressive fort there, so the

Mongols employed their trebuchets and the Chuangzi-Nu, a clever wooden and metal device that could shoot volleys of burning arrows at the enemy. They also used what were called "thunder crash bombs," metal cylinders filled with gunpowder. The Mongols were successful in this battle, and they were ultimately successful in the war against the Song. By 1279, the Song dynasty was no more.

The "Last" Song Emperor

The moral character of Emperor Lizong, who assumed the throne in 1224, was deplorable. He was self-indulgent and blind to the growing threat of the Mongols, who had already attacked and conquered some of the Jin lands to the north.

Lizong had no sons of his own, so he decided to adopt his nephew, Duzong, and ready him to be the heir to the throne. However, Duzong had developmental difficulties and limited intelligence because his mother had tried to abort him when she was pregnant, and the medical procedures she underwent were crude.

Duzong held the throne from 1264 to 1274. Courtiers felt pity for Emperor Duzong, as he was physically and mentally incapable of his role. In fact, Duzong heard about the Mongols and the Battle of Xiangyang from a palace maid. When Duzong asked a Song chancellor, Jia Sidao, about the attack, the man tried to hide it from him in a misguided effort at compassion.

Duzong was not technically the last emperor of the Song dynasty. However, many historians view him as the last one because he was the last emperor who could have made a real change in stopping the Mongols' advancement.

Chapter 6 – Kublai Khan: The Yuan Dynasty, 1271–1368

Kublai Khan was the grandson of Genghis Khan. When he was younger, he had studied Chinese philosophy and Buddhist teachings from Haiyun, a Buddhist monk, as well as a more advanced form of Buddhism under Drogon Chogyal Phagpa, a revered teacher of Buddhism. In 1252, Kublai was in charge of the territories in northern China that the Mongols had captured. While there, he learned mathematics and astronomy from the well-known Zhao Bi who lived there. In 1260, after the death of Mongke Khan, Kublai became the new ruler of the Mongol Empire.

Kublai Khan was not only a great leader and fighter, but he was also an excellent writer and poet. His narrative, *Ascent to Spring Mountain*, contains fascinating nature motifs and deep thoughts, such as, "Flowers shone bright rays and auspicious colors gleamed like a rainbow. Incense smoke wafted like mist and a blessed light emanated."

In 1271, the year the Mongols overran the Song dynasty, Kublai Khan announced the advent of a new dynasty known as Yuan. In the city of Shangdu, also known as Xanadu, Kublai built his summer palace, which is located in present-day Inner Mongolia. In 1275, the

Italian explorer Marco Polo described it as "the palace of the Great Khan, [is] the most extensive that has ever been known. The sides of the great halls are adorned with dragons in carved wood and gold, figures of warriors, of birds and of beasts. On each of the sides of the palace are grand flights of marble steps."

There were parks and grazing lands, on which Kublai kept a herd of special white horses, the Mongolian horse, a recognized breed today. It is a very hardy horse, accustomed to frigid temperatures and hard travel. These horses were ideal for battle. Mongolian cavalrymen could ride these horses without saddles by gripping the animal's sides with their legs alone.

Kublai Khan was fond of great feasts and enjoyed the entertainment of magicians from other lands. Marco Polo tried to figure out their act, saying that they were carried out by the use of helpers in the crowd. These magicians could raise glasses in the air without being held.

Religious tolerance was practiced throughout the realm. Kublai Khan respected the practices of Christians, Jews, Buddhists, shamans, Taoists, and Muslims.

War against Japan

The great Khan had an intense interest in widening his empire and sent out military expeditions with the purpose of invading Japan, Vietnam, Java, and Burma.

In 1281, Kublai Khan invaded Japan. He had an excellent Mongol navy, which he utilized by sending out 3,500 ships from southern China into the harbors of Japan. He sent out two fleets, with one fleet taking an easterly route and the other taking a southern one. However, the eastern fleet failed to follow orders and wait for the southern fleet to join up with them. Instead, the eastern fleet attacked mainland Japan alone.

As one might expect, their attempt to invade Japan went terribly. Many Mongols were either killed, wounded, or ended up in slavery. Japan was able to stay isolated, as they kicked the Mongols out of the waters surrounding their islands.

Battles in Dai Viet (Vietnam)

There were three great battles initiated by the Yuan dynasty to gain control of Dai Viet. In 1257, the Mongols subdued the Tran clan of Dai Viet, and it became a vassal state that had to pay tribute. However, when the Yuan asked to march through Tran territory in order to gain access to the south (South Vietnam), the Tran king refused. Insulted, the Mongolians demanded their surrender, which the Tran refused. So, in 1284, the Yuan attacked Dai Viet and won. After the Tran surrendered, they decided not to go ahead with a peace treaty. Instead, the Tran attacked the Mongols, and they proved to be victorious.

In 1285, the Mongols attacked again. This time, the soldiers of Dai Viet obtained the help of a neighboring khan, Duwa of the Chagatai Khanate. He assisted the Dai Viet soldiers and defeated Kublai's soldiers at a garrison in the Tarim Basin.

In 1287, the Mongols attempted to invade Dai Viet once more. This time, they achieved a partial victory and occupied some land near Ha Long Bay. However, the Tran general, Tran Khanh Du, destroyed the Mongolian supply ships. Bereft of supplies, the Mongols were forced to retreat the following year.

Invasions of Burma

The battles between the Yuan dynasty and Burma dragged on and off for nearly ten years, between 1277 and 1287. While the Mongols had been able to subdue them early on, they had a difficult time collecting tributes and had to return frequently to demand them. Unknown to the Mongols, the tiny kingdoms of the land were constantly restive. In addition, the Burmese were mostly farmers who had endured several droughts.

In 1287, when a treaty was drawn up, the king of Burma was assassinated. He had been accused of abandoning his people to the Mongols. In their histories, King Narathihapate was then called "the king who fled from the Taruk."

Society and Welfare Programs

Kublai Khan organized society according to ethnic groups. He did so to keep Mongolians in the top positions of power during his reign. The order would have gone something like this: 1) Mongols, 2) central Asians (non-Chinese), 3) northern Chinese, and 4) southern Chinese.

However, he was merciful and believed in fairness. After he conquered the country of Burma, he discovered that there was great poverty, especially among those who were ill or unable to support their families. To the regions with the greatest need, he sent grain and cloth for making clothing. He also had construction workers from his lands help repair homes in cases of disasters, such as floods and wars. In addition, he asked that farmers donate their time and skills if farms in those afflicted areas had needs like sowing, harvesting, or digging irrigation channels.

Death of Chabi and Kublai

Some of Kublai's imperial princes joined together in rebellion, and they attempted to gain land and wealth for themselves. Corruption crept into the government, and Kublai was powerless to control it, as large parts of the empire in the 13th century defied central control.

In 1281, Kublai's favorite wife, Chabi, died, and he became despondent. As Kublai reflected on his past life, his failures to subjugate Japan and Dai Viet occupied his mind, making him even more depressed. Likewise, he was unable to control the corruption in the government and the resentment of the peasants, as they were being overtaxed.

In 1287, Nayan's Rebellion triggered constant unrest in the Manchuria districts, and variations of that revolt haunted him for years. In 1294, Kublai Khan died at the age of seventy-eight.

Ma Zhiyuan (pen name: Dongli), a Yuan poet, wrote of Kublai Khan, saying, "A withered vine, an ancient tree, crows at dusk. A little bridge, a flowing stream. An old road, wind out of the west, an emaciated horse. On the horizon at sunset is a broken-hearted man."

The Decline of the Yuan

Unlike the Chinese emperors before him, Kublai Khan's rise wasn't marred with fratricide and murder. However, the strife and challenges of managing China tore away at the fabric of society. Despite the lack of internecine violence, discrimination against the Han Chinese by Kublai Khan and the Mongolian overlords made its mark, as vital governmental positions were always given to Mongolians, while the Chinese held lesser posts. Because the Han was the major ethnic group in mainland China, this prejudice eventually bred violence.

The Red Turban Rebellions

Many of the Han Chinese turned to their religious roots in Buddhism, seeking solace from the growing prejudice of the Mongols. In the 13th century, the White Lotus movement, which followed the belief in the coming of a savior, Buddha Maitreya, triggered revolts against Mongolian rule. When the White Lotus organization was banned, they went underground.

In 1351, the White Lotus movement spawned what was called the Red Turban Rebellion. They were so-named because they wore red scarves and red turbans. The Red Turbans formed an official army and attacked Mongol officials indiscriminately. A powerful leader by the name of Zhu Yuanzhang rose from this movement, and he would go on to found the next dynasty of China.

While the infrastructure of the Yuan dynasty was crumbling due to the rebellions, plague struck. Millions of people died; it is estimated that in the 14th century, 30 percent of the population of China died from the disease. Thus, the Yuan dynasty lost its support, and it succumbed to the ravages of violence and disease.

Chapter 7 – The Great Ming Dynasty, 1368–1644

The Hongwu Emperor

In 1368, Zhu Yuanzhang, the hallowed victor of the Red Turban Rebellion, became the first emperor of the Ming dynasty. He took on the era name of "Hongwu," meaning "vastly martial." The use of era names had been used since 140 BCE, but the Hongwu Emperor introduced the tradition of having only one era name for each ruler; before this, rulers could change their era name as many times as they pleased.

So far, Chinese history had been characterized by a repetitious pattern of conspiracies, murders, betrayals, and corruption. Hongwu was a man familiar with all of that, and these aspects manifested under his own rule. He conducted frequent purges of his administration and even his own staff of servants. Some historians report that Hongwu's paranoia resulted in as many as 30,000 executions. The country had many military garrisons, especially along its borders, but Hongwu didn't give his generals much authority to make independent decisions. Hongwu also adopted a legal code fashioned after Confucian philosophy. Confucius was noted as being a leader who placed a heavy emphasis on obedience to authority, so a Confucian legal code was a logical outcome of such thinking.

The Mongols, who had ruled prior to the Ming dynasty, were scrupulously controlled. During the Yuan era, the Han Chinese were the victims of prejudice, so this might be considered a case of reverse discrimination.

The Miao Revolts

Southern China, in the 1370s, was a rebellious area, especially Yunnan province, just north of Burma. The native people there resisted the Ming-style of governance, and in doing so, they represented a threat to the emperor's authoritarian regime. In order to control these violent outbreaks, which were referred to as the Miao revolts, Hongwu recruited the Uyghur people from the northwestern provinces of China. The Uyghur forces suppressed these rebellions, but revolts later broke out again in the 15th century. The Ming emperor was able to put the rebellions down again, albeit doing so in cruel ways. For instance, in 1460, the Ming emperor called for the castration of over 1,500 Miao boys, some of whom died in the process. Those that survived were turned into eunuch slaves.

Eventually, many of the Uyghurs migrated to Hunan in central China. These people were referred to as Hui Chinese, the majority of whom practiced Islam.

The Manchurian Sector

In Manchuria, in north-central China, most of the people were descendants of the Jurchens, who were troublesome nomads. The Hongwu Emperor didn't desire close relations with them, and his administration had little political presence in the area, with the exception of posted guards and garrisons to quell local unrest. This would change over time, with later Ming emperors interested in controlling the area more fully.

The Tibetans

In Tibet, the Hongwu Emperor granted the people semi-autonomy. They were (and still are) fervent Buddhists, ranging among four different Buddhist sects. The predominant sect is the Gelug,

"Yellow Hats," which is led by a leader called the Dalai Lama. Today's head of Tibetan Buddhism, Tenzin Gyatso, is the 14th Dalai Lama. Historically, the Tibetans had the protection of the Mongols, which tended to dissuade the Hongwu Emperor and other Ming emperors from creating close relations with them.

The Yongle Emperor

Although the Hongwu Emperor named his grandson, Zhu Yuwen, as his successor, his son, Zhu Di, was consumed with jealousy and set off a three-year civil war during which he had his nephew, his nephew's wife, his aunt, and the palace courtiers killed. Zhu then proclaimed himself to be the Yongle Emperor in 1402.

The Forbidden City

The Forbidden City is a complex of imperial palaces, administrative buildings, worship areas, and residences for the palace personnel and widowed empresses from prior years.

The Yongle Emperor established the capital at current-day Beijing in 1420, which was where he started building the Forbidden City in 1406. It is the crowning achievement of his reign. The Forbidden City is so named because only the emperor, his immediate family, and his eunuch servants were supposedly allowed to enter unless the emperor had given his express permission otherwise. The ancillary outer buildings served administrative functions, so those were places where other officials and state visitors could enter and perform their duties.

This magnificent structure has 980 rooms. There is a 171-foot moat around it, as well as a myriad of thick defensive walls. The artisans imitated the building styles they saw in the silk paintings of the Song dynasty. There are elaborate gateways on all four sides bearing the names "Gate of Divine Might," "East Glorious Gate," West Glorious Gate," "Dongan Gate," "East and West Chang'an Gates," and "Meridian Gate." Many of the inner buildings carry inspirational names like "Hall of Supreme Harmony," "Palace of Heavenly Purity," "Hall of Earthly Tranquility," and "Hall of Universal Happiness."

The roofs in the Forbidden City were made with yellow-glazed tiles and decorated with lines of statuettes with imperial dragons, phoenixes, and the like. The walls are punctuated with reliefs, mandalas, paintings, and icons. Themes are derived from Taoism, but there are some areas manifesting shamanism or Buddhist beliefs.

Treasure Voyages

The Yongle Emperor wanted to impress the countries near China with the wealth of the Ming dynasty in order to discourage invasions and project the enormous power of the Ming. Starting in 1403, he had his admiral, Zheng He, order the construction of fleets of impressive ships. They were heavily armored and carried artistic creations, silks, clothing with gold brocade, and a collection of supplies. The Chinese gave these treasures as gifts to the heads and representatives of foreign governments. They then invited dignitaries and ambassadors from various countries to visit them in China. Because of this unexpected generosity, some of the other countries were willing to become tributary states in exchange for military defense.

On their first voyage in 1405, they went to Champa (Vietnam), Java, Malacca (Malay), Aru (Indonesia), Semudera (Sumatra), Ceylon (Sri Lanka), and other islands and lands in the South Pacific. On their way back to China, Zheng He and his crew had to confront the pirate Chen Zuyi. For years, the pirates had monopolized the seas around Sumatra and raided ships of other island countries. The Chinese attacked the pirates' vessels and took Chen Zuyi and three other pirates back to China, where they were executed in 1407. The people of Sumatra, in particular, were grateful. That encounter opened up navigation channels south of Indonesia and its environs.

In 1407, the Yongle Emperor continued his treasure voyages. Most of the time, relations were cordial. However, on their second expedition to Java, some Chinese ambassadors were killed. The people of western Java were insulted that the Chinese first paid respects to their enemies in eastern Java, and they took it out on the visiting Chinese. The two were at a crossroads because of a civil war that hadn't been entirely resolved. After the civil war had ended, the king of western Java sent envoys to China on an apology tour, and relations were reestablished.

On their third voyage in 1409, the Chinese visited many of the islands they had seen before, but they also toured Ceylon (Sri Lanka) and ports in southern India. Ceylon and its ruler, King Alagakkonara, had a local reputation for threatening small neighboring island regimes that had diplomatic relations with China. As might be expected, Alagakkonara attacked the Chinese fleet. Zheng. He responded by disembarking troops at their capital city of Kotte and captured it. They then kidnapped the king and carried him back to China. The Yongle Emperor decided to release him. The event was recorded by the chronicler Yang Rong, who called the people of Ceylon "insignificant worms" and wrote, "the august emperor spared their lives, and they humbly kowtowed, making crude sounds, and praised the sage-like virtue of the Ming ruler."

The Yongle Emperor freed the king of Ceylon, not to show his magnanimity but rather his power and influence. In 1411, he had King Alagakkonara deposed and placed a pro-Chinese king on the throne.

On the fourth voyage, which took place between 1413 and 1415, Zheng He and his men meddled in the affairs of the island of Sumatra. They deposed a man who had usurped the throne of Sumatra and had him transported back to China, where he was executed. Following that, Sumatra made generous annual tributes to China in gratitude.

During the fourth journey, there are records, which are backed up by archeological evidence, that indicate the Chinese treasure voyages traveled as far as the Strait of Hormuz in the Persian Gulf.

In 1419, the fifth treasure voyage sailed to the Gulf of Aden in Yemen near the Red Sea. The tributes the Chinese received after their voyages there included exotic animals such as leopards, rhinoceroses, camels, zebras, and even ostriches.

On their sixth voyage in 1421, the Chinese fleet left with envoys from Aden and Siam (Thailand). They most likely saw a small portion of the noteworthy Grand Canal before arriving at the imperial court in Beijing. The Yongle Emperor had recalled the treasure fleet to protect Beijing because hostilities were heating up between Ming China and the Mongols.

The Yongle Emperor died in 1424. After his death, China progressively started to withdraw from the world stage and became increasingly isolated.

The Tumu Crisis

After having lost their power in China, the Mongols were resentful. This continued to spur hatred and violence.

In 1449, things came to a head. The Yongle Emperor's great-grandson and descendant, the Zhengtong Emperor, who came to power in 1435, was captured by Mongol rebels at a battle outside the Tumu Fortress, which abutted Mongol territories. Although emperors didn't usually lead troops into battle, his eunuch advisor, Weng Zhen, encouraged him to do so. It was a disaster.

Esen Taishi, the leader of the Mongols, planned on getting a hefty ransom for the emperor's release and some profitable arrangements in terms of trade. The Ming officials refused to pay the ransom or negotiate, and so, Esen's efforts failed. Esen antagonized his forces with that failure, and they assassinated him in retaliation. The Mongols held the Zhengtong Emperor for a year, during which time the Zhengtong Emperor abdicated in favor of his younger brother, who became the Jingtai Emperor. Regardless of the fact that there was no trade deal and no ransom, the Mongols still fared quite well, having purloined many weapons and gear from the dead Chinese warriors.

When the Mongols released Zhengtong, Chinese officials immediately placed him under house arrest, and he stayed there for almost seven years. In 1457, Zhengtong deposed the Jingtai Emperor and assumed the role of emperor once more, now calling himself the Tianshun Emperor.

Retaking the imperial throne wasn't an easy move for the Tianshun Emperor. Because the imperial forces under General Cao Qin had failed to prevent the kidnapping of the emperor, Cao was afraid he himself might be executed. After all, Cao's non-Chinese forces were Mongols who were loyal to the Ming. Even though those Mongols were aligned with the Ming, their ethnicity alone made them look guilty.

On account of the incident, Lu Gao of the imperial house was sent to investigate the role of Cao Qin. Cao couldn't let that happen, so he decapitated Lu Gao and dismembered his body. He then took Lu's severed head to the grand secretary of the regime, Li Xian, and lied to him, saying that it was Lu Gao himself who was planning the rebellion. Li Xian didn't believe him, so Cao stole some paper from Li Xian's office and wrote a message to the emperor, claiming Cao was innocent. No one allowed that note to go through to the emperor. No doubt they felt it was a subterfuge. Cao now felt he had only one option: unseat the Tianshun Emperor in a coup.

Cao Qin's Rebellion

In 1461, Cao and his men entered the Forbidden City, attacked Dongan Gate and East and West Chang'an Gates. They set fire to the two Chang'an Gates and raced inside. General Sun Tang of the Imperial Guard and his soldiers stormed in. Cao's forces killed two of them and fled outside the walls to Dongan Gate. The imperial soldiers killed some of Cao's men, including his brother. He and his men then retreated and tried to escape through the gate on the outer wall. Many of his men escaped into the city.

Like a frightened boy, Cao ran to his own home and threw up makeshift defensive walls and objects. Once the imperial troops under Sun Tang broke in, Cao threw himself down a deep well on his property and died. The warriors hoisted up his body, dismembered it, and put it on public display in Beijing.

Cao's men were eventually rounded up. Some seemed to have been coerced into the rebellion or were misled into believing it was something else. These men were released or given lesser sentences, while others involved were sentenced to death. From that point on, any Mongols who served in the army were given desk posts elsewhere or were forced to retire. A program was then started to relocate the Mongols living inside the empire. Many were sent to remote places with uncomfortable climatic conditions.

From Exploration to Isolation

In 1479, the Ministry of War burned the written records of Zheng He's treasure voyages. Regulations spewed forth from the administration, restricting the sizes of new ships to be built and specifying the military functions of such vessels. Ships were docked until they rotted from disuse.

This seems like a radical thing to do. After all, the huge, well-armed Chinese ships decreased incidents of piracy, especially in the South Pacific. Zheng He and his sailors had annihilated pirate vessels and discouraged others from raiding the cities of defenseless island nations. This all changed, though, when China started to withdraw from the world stage.

After the treasure voyages of the Yongle Emperor, there was a great backlash in China against the rise of international trade and goodwill missions to neighboring countries. For years, historians and political commentators have argued about the possible causes for that.

One theory has to do with social class rivalry. The nobles and elites within the top circles of the administration were overprotective of their influence. The increase of trade was a threat to them because it brought wealth and importance to the rising merchant class. Instead of allowing free trade, the government monopolized foreign trade. As a result, the mercantile class objected to governmental control. They did yield some power because shipping and mercantilism have a nearly symbiotic relationship. In the 15th century, China had 3,500 ships—more than that of the US Navy today!

The costs of Zheng He's treasure voyages between 1407 to 1433 was another possible reason for the cessation of regular voyages. They were expensive and required many funds from the nation's treasury to supply and maintain the ships. Some argue that they weren't that profitable, as the net income was negligible.

In addition, there was internal strife caused by the rebellions related to the Mongols. The Chinese navy was useless in those struggles since they occurred within the country itself.

Competition also existed between court officials and the eunuchs who were close to the emperor. The eunuchs preferred international trade, but the reasons for that preference is vague. Some historians indicate that it gave the eunuchs an opportunity to siphon profits for themselves.

The Ming rulers were sometimes called xenophobes, but they did pull back on some of the "alien" cultural practices that existed during the former Yuan dynasty. The first emperor—the Hongwu Emperor—required Muslim women to marry Han Chinese men in order to become more Sinicized. He did have more mosques built and permitted Islam to be practiced.

Generally, the non-Han Chinese people that came into China during the prior Yuan dynasty were encouraged to assimilate into the culture of the Han Chinese, which was, and still is, the largest of the ethnic Chinese population. In time, the isolation of the Ming necessarily resulted in the integration of non-Chinese into China.

European Contact

The Portuguese were renowned for being traders, and they had made contact with almost all of the significant countries in the East and the West. In 1517, a merchant vessel visited the city of Guangzhou, and King Manuel I of Portugal sent a delegation to the court of the Zhengde Emperor, who ruled from 1505 to 1521.

Malacca, in Indonesia, which Zheng He had visited during the treasure voyages, sent their ambassadors to see the succeeding Jiajing Emperor. The Indonesians were jealous of the Portuguese and started circulating rumors that the Portuguese kidnapped Chinese children and ate them! Through fear, the Ming navy refused to allow the Portuguese to land at Tuen Mun (near Hong Kong) in 1521 and did so again in 1522.

The Ningbo Incident

In 1523, Japan sent a vessel into the harbor of Ningbo bearing gifts and products for the Chinese emperor and his people. They had made contact with the Zhengde Emperor prior to that, but he had passed away by the time the Japanese delegation arrived. Japan only made these tribute journeys once every ten years, but it was very profitable for the Chinese, so the Jiajing Emperor agreed to receive them.

However, a massive squabble broke out that accelerated into violence. It seems that two Japanese delegations—the Hosokawa delegation and the Ouchi delegation—both came. When the Hosokawa clan was received ahead of the Ouchi, they drew swords. The head of the Hosokawa delegation was killed, and his ship was set on fire in the port. The Japanese warriors then disembarked, overran Ningbo, and plundered randomly. They even commandeered a Chinese ship, kidnapped the head of a garrison in Ningbo, and made off to sea with him. They were chased by a fleet of Ming vessels, but the Ouchi managed to defeat them.

Only two more Japanese trade missions followed: one in 1540 and another in 1549. The Jiajing Emperor was on the throne by this time, and he was a very isolated person. His preference for privacy spilled over into his regime, and he discontinued the Chinese-Japanese trade. China had already been pursuing a policy of isolation, but it only increased under the Jiajing Emperor.

The problem became more critical when Chinese merchants started setting up illegal trade in some of the more remote islands in the South Pacific. This ceased when some of these merchants ran into debt, creating embarrassing incidents involving China and Japan.

The Wokou Raids

Wokou means "dwarf pirates" in English. It was an insulting term used by the Chinese to refer to the Japanese. The wokou (Japanese pirates) continued to conduct illegal trade with Chinese merchants as they had done during the regime of the Jiajing Emperor. Because this overseas trade was banned by the Ming dynasty, many Chinese and

Japanese merchants moved their bases of operation to the islands off the coasts of China and Japan.

Xu Hai was one of the most notable merchant-pirates, and he operated out of Malacca, which was one of the Indonesian islands explored by Zheng He. Wang Zhi was another Chinese pirate who was bold enough to work off of the island of Kyushu, located off the coast of southern Japan.

In 1547, the Portuguese partook in the piracy when they plundered Zhangzhou. A general named Zhu Wan was then appointed as the Superintendent of Military Affairs, and it was his responsibility to put an end to the piracy and illegal off-land trade. In 1549, his commander, Lu Tang, grabbed two Chinese junks operating illegally in the waters off of Zoumaxi. Zhu Wan took it upon himself to execute 96 Chinese smugglers. The Jiajing Emperor was furious, as Zhu Wan had acted on his accord instead of following protocol, and called for his arrest. Zhu Wan, however, committed suicide rather than be taken captive.

The empire went through a succession of commanders and lesser officials in charge of eradicating the pirate activities, including Zhang Jing, Hu Zongxian, Zhou Chang, and Yang Yi. They achieved only limited success, and cruel executions resulted. For instance, in 1555, it was reported that 1,900 pirates had been beheaded. Despite this impressive number, the emperor was unimpressed by the delays in their attacks, and as a result, the chief commander, Zhang Jing, was beheaded.

When Hu Zongxian became supreme commander in 1556, he was in favor of opening up trade—a move that would reduce piracy. He sent envoys to Japan to enlist their cooperation. Hu Zongxian also contacted the pirate Wang Zhi, hoping to reduce violence through appeasement. Wang Zhi, however, refused.

While making an effort to change how things were done, Hu was outwitted by a rogue pirate, Xu Hai. In 1556, Xu disembarked thousands of warriors on mainland China, who plundered the city of Zaolin. The city's defenders were initially successful in driving them away, but their reinforcements didn't arrive in time, and China lost the battle.

Even though he was wounded, Xu Hai had his pirate raiders move into the city of Tongxiang and place it under siege. The city resisted strongly, and the fact that they had a formidable defensive wall kept them alive. However, morale was very low after a month had passed.

Hu Zongxian then contacted Xu Hai to make a peace agreement with him. As a show of goodwill, the pirate released 200 Chinese prisoners. The emperor and the pirate reached an agreement, and the pirates withdrew. Hu then convinced Xu Hai to change sides and then had Xu himself eliminate some of the Japanese pirates.

As Xu continued eliminating pirates, chaos erupted. Other pirates had arrived and were scrambling to confiscate each other's booty. The Chinese navy descended upon the pirates and wiped them out, with the exception of the pirate Chen Dong, who was captured. Chen Dong was brought to Jiaxing, where he was executed.

In the meantime, the Jiajing Emperor notified Commander Hu that no surrender would be accepted. Instead, he preferred not to take prisoners, and he also wished to maintain his isolationist policy. He had no wish to negotiate with pirates or with the non-Chinese people, and he did not want to inaugurate any form of foreign trade.

Hu Zongxian then realized he needed to change his position about making trade agreements with the pirates. Hu Zongxian decided to trick another major pirate, Wang Zhi, into thinking he had a peace agreement. When Wang Zhi arrived, he was imprisoned and executed.

Wang Zhi's followers then reorganized, moved south to Fujian, and continued with the raids. A large island base was created in the Kinmen island chain, but there were far fewer pirates than there had been.

General Qi Jiguang took over after Hu Zongxian. He developed a new military formation and even wrote about it in the *New Treatise on Military Efficiency*. Qi's strategy was extremely effective and totally unanticipated by the raiders, and due to his efforts, and that of Hu before him, piracy was no longer considered a major threat.

The Shaanxi Earthquake

In 1556, the deadliest earthquake on record hit Shaanxi province in central China. It reverberated in the neighboring provinces of Henan, Hebei, Hunan, Shandong, Jiangsu, and Anhui. Around 520 miles was destroyed by the impact, and current estimates indicate that it hit either a 7.9 or an 8 on the Mercalli scale. Many people in Shaanxi lived in artificial caves, called yaodongs, which were hewn in loess cliffs. Loess is sediment made up of wind-blown dirt. It has a very low clay content, making it unstable and prone to crumbling. Due to this, the cliffs collapsed when the earthquake struck. Around 830,000 people died in the Shaanxi earthquake. Because China had isolated itself, it alone had to carry the burden, and the catastrophe had a devastating effect on the Chinese economy.

Trade Concessions

After a long period of isolation and cessation of trade, China acquiesced to the gentle persuasion of the Portuguese, who returned again in 1553. They dispelled some of the rumors and attempted to repair their reputation that had been sullied, and because of their efforts, the port of Macau was opened up to Portuguese trade in 1557.

Due to the Wokou raids that haunted the islands and ports of southern China, relations between China and Japan were frozen. Japanese merchants used the Portuguese as intermediaries so they could obtain silk, which they exchanged for Japanese silver. Spain became involved in trade with China after that and purchased not only silver and silk but also the fine porcelain for which the Ming dynasty was noted. Porcelain became a major export to Europe and Japan.

Ming Porcelain

The Ming artisans were famous for their exquisite porcelain items, such as vases, bowls, urns, cups, and incense burners. It was more translucent than porcelain from other countries, as the Chinese used kaolin (a white clay) for the body of the object and secured coloring agents by using cobalt oxide from minerals. Other colors, which were used less frequently, were red, yellow, and green. By the 16th century, many pieces were multi-colored. Kilns around the country spewed smoke into the sky and even created a fog-like cloud over Jingdezhen, one of the towns recognized for its art community. Today, Ming porcelain is prized on the antique markets.

An Explosion Predicts the Demise of the Ming Dynasty

On May 30th, 1626, Beijing was rocked by a massive explosion. Naked bodies fell from the air, their clothes obliterated by the blast. Uprooted trees landed miles away. The sky went black, and body parts of people and animals rained down upon the ground for miles around. The roof tiles of the Forbidden City and nearby residences became lethal projectiles, shooting into people on the streets and in their houses. About 20,000 people died.

The cause was reportedly an explosion at the Wanggongchang Armory, which manufactured gunpowder, weapons, and munitions. It was also a storage facility for hundreds of explosives. However, it should be noted that the exact cause of the explosion has never been determined. While the most likely theory is that it was started by the facility, that doesn't explain the lack of damage around the facility itself or the fact that people's clothing just flew off their bodies.

Many believed the explosion was a sign from the gods that they disapproved of the current Tianqi Emperor and his administration. The fact that the emperor also lost his son in the blast bolstered that opinion.

The Tianqi Emperor issued gold to be used for relief efforts. However, China was already in a state of financial collapse. Peasants were starving, and soldiers mutinied. Massive bands of rebels wandered the streets, no longer afraid of reprisals by imperial soldiers. The Tianqi Emperor died a year after the Wanggongchang explosion, and his brother took over, becoming the Chongzhen Emperor in 1627. Little did he know that a new dynasty was starting to form right before his eyes.

The Jurchens Return!

The Jurchens were now more sophisticated and had evolved from their nomadic roots. They had settled in Manchuria and were now called the Manchu. They were also referred to as the "red-tasseled Manchus."

While the last Ming emperor was still on the throne, the Manchu State flourished. Nurhaci, who grew up in a Chinese household, was the one responsible for uniting the various Jurchen tribes into the Manchu. He was learned but had the fire of youth and idealism. As early as 1616, he had united the Han Bannermen and the Eight Banners, which consisted mostly of Manchu people. He then proceeded to unite many of the Jurchen tribes. There were activist organizations throughout China, such as the Eight Banners, the Shun rebels, the Jurchens, and, in 1644, the Green Standard Army. Leaders rose and fell, as these groups culled out useless members and merged into more cohesive units.

Nurhaci was courageous, and he was dedicated to laying the foundation for a truly meaningful administration. To show his determination, he presented the Ming dynasty with a document called the *Seven Grievances*. This was tantamount to a declaration of war. The grievances are briefly listed here with explanations where needed:

> 1. The Ming slaughtered Nurhaci's father and grandfather without cause. (Nurhaci's father, Taksi, and his grandfather, Giocangga, were killed by Nikan Wailan, a Jurchen working as an operative for a Ming general.)
>
> 2. The Ming oppressed the Jianzhou (Jurchen clan) and favored two other clans, the Hada and Yehe.
>
> 3. The Ming violated the agreement made with Nurhaci in the past. (The Ming agreed to have marked borders between Ming lands and lands settled by the tribes, but the Ming ignored the agreement. The Ming also gave Nurhaci the power to regulate Jurchen activities and commerce but then undermined him.)

4. The Ming sent forces to protect the Yehe clan in their conflicts with the Jianzhou. (The Ming had agreed *not* to interfere with Nurhaci's duties. It was Nurhaci's responsibility to protect the Yehe.)

5. The Ming supported the Yehe and encouraged them to break their promise to Nurhaci. (The Ming saw to it that Nurhaci's fiancé was married off to the leader of the Yehe rather than to Nurhaci as they had agreed.)

6. The Ming forces forbade Nurhaci from harvesting crops from the lands he owned in three provinces.

7. The Ming garrison official, Shang Bozhi, was given free rein and abused his position.

In 1644, the Green Standard Amy, a paramilitary organization, was created. It consisted mainly of Han soldiers. All were required to adopt the queue, a Manchu hairstyle, by which a man has the top of his head shaven and braids the hair at the back of his head into a tail. Those who followed Confucius disliked it, as it says in Confucius's writings, "A person's body and hair, being gifts from one's parents, should not be damaged." Even though the Han Chinese were averse to it, they did it because the punishment for not doing so was death.

Nurhaci's efforts spread to the Liaodong Peninsula, which contains Beijing. He needed as many supporters as he could get from that region. He attracted many Mongols, who had been suppressed by the Ming dynasty. Many Ming soldiers, who deplored the heartless practices of their own administration, defected and joined with the Eight Bannermen. The Jurchens, who were absorbed within this union, were never referred to as the "Jurchens" in the military records. This was because the name "Jurchen" conjured up the image of an unclean nomadic savage.

Nurhaci died in 1626 and was succeeded by his eighth son, Hong Taiji. Hong Taiji continued where his father left off, preparing for an armed assault of the Ming dynasty. One of his earliest accomplishments was the development of a cannon, which was fashioned after the European-style one. He used Ming metallurgists to build it and trained fighters to become accomplished artillerymen. Gunpowder weaponry was also made, along with muskets.

Hong Taiji also planned on having an organized administration, so he would have officials in place as needed. It was similar to the Ming form of government. Also, like the Ming, the new dynasty would use traditional protocols in order to gain the confidence of the people.

The Demise of the Ming Dynasty

The Chongzhen Emperor was naïve and grossly incompetent. The country's structure and government were, by then, only ghosts of what they once were. He didn't know how to handle the *Seven Grievances* of Nurhaci, and he knew he couldn't keep the Ming dynasty intact. Because the rebellions and various militant groups were out of control, the Chongzhen Emperor despaired. In 1644, he walked into his imperial garden and hung himself from a tree. His suicide note read, "I die, unable to face my ancestors in the underworld, dejected and ashamed."

Chapter 8 –The Rise of the Qing, 1636–1912

Hong Taiji died in 1643 before the Qing could entirely unite China. After his death, Hong's five-year-old son was looked at as the next successor, and a group of men declared that he had the Mandate of Heaven. He became the Shunzhi Emperor, but Hong Taiji's half-brother, Dorgon, held most of the power, as he was the regent.

His aim was conformity among the people, so, in 1645, he passed an edict dictating that the queue hairstyle was an obligation for all males. To him, it was a sign of loyalty, and Dorgon had a compulsive need for uniformity. Massive executions resulted from non-compliance with the queue requirement. Even some of the native Han Chinese carried these out, but they were done so under the orders of Dorgon.

In 1650, Dorgon died in a hunting expedition. Many hated him so much that they disinterred his body and mutilated it to pay for his "crimes." In 1662, after Dorgon's death, the Shunzhi assumed control. He had been very much aware of the hostility engendered by his predecessors and wanted a kinder, gentler administration to come about. He made attempted to ferret out the corruption, although it had long been entrenched.

To address the diverse ethnic groups within the Qing dynasty, Shunzhi's advisors had people use terms for him that coincided with their historical practice. For instance, in Tibet, he was called "Gong Ma"; in Mongolia, he was called "Bogda Khan"; in the Manchu regions, he was called "Huangdi," meaning "emperor," or "Khan," if people preferred that.

Revolt of the Three Feudatories

In 1655, there were three fiefdoms set up in China, the joint provinces of Yunnan and Guizhou, Fujian, and Guangdong.

Military commander Wu Sangui was placed in charge of the joint southwestern provinces of Yunnan and Guizhou. He was also assigned to serve as a liaison to the Dalai Lama, who lived in the region.

In Fujian province on the east coast, Geng Jingzhong was the ruler. Geng was tyrannical and, unknown to the emperor, established the practice of extorting money from his own people. His son replaced him in 1682 when Geng died. Unfortunately, he was very much like his father, so little changed.

Shang Zhixin was in charge of Guangdong province after his father, Shang Kexi, stepped down in 1673. Like Geng, the two of them were autocratic.

The Kangxi Emperor noted that those provinces, when put together, managed to spend half of the nation's treasure. In order to draw their attention to the fact that they might be monitored, the Kangxi Emperor reduced their powers and watched them carefully. The three generals, although they were quite capable, were all very headstrong and arrogant.

In 1667, Wu Sangui asked to retire. In 1673, both Geng Jingzhong and Shang Kexi followed suit. This was a curious coincidence. A conspiracy was afoot, but the Kangxi Emperor didn't suspect anything.

Civil War

In 1673, Wu Sangui declared a new dynasty of his own, the Zhou Dynasty, named after the former pre-imperial Zhou dynasty. His call was for the restoration of the Ming rule, and he incited the Han

Chinese to join him by promising to repeal the order about wearing the queues. Soon after this declaration, Wu Sangui attacked and captured Sichuan and Hunan in central China.

The following year, Geng Jingzhong took over Fujian, and Shang Kexi, along with his son, Shang Zhixin, annexed Guangdong. Then, Sun Yanling, Wang Fuchen, and Zheng Jing, who were also powerful generals, joined the revolt and confiscated the lands of Guangxi, Shaanxi, Tungning, Yunnan, and Zhejiang.

The Qing forces were loyal to the Kangxi Emperor and were tough warriors. The Han Green Standard Army, along with miscellaneous Manchu and Mongol forces, started dispelling the rebels in 1676. Wang Fuchen surrendered in the northwest regions. In 1678, Wu Sangui murdered his rival, Sun Yanling, and died that same year himself. His grandson, Wu Shifan, took over, but he eventually retreated and later committed suicide. Sichuan and Shaanxi were reclaimed by the Qing troops, along with Guangxi. Shang Zhixin survived the conflict in Guangdong but was forced to commit suicide in 1680. Zheng Jing's warriors were forced to withdraw and retreated back to Taiwan. Zheng died, and his son surrendered in his name in 1683.

The Qing dynasty acquired Taiwan by default because some of the rebels had annexed the island, although they hadn't set out to do that initially.

Because it was so widespread, the rebellion was very costly. During the rule of the Kangxi Emperor, he made allowances for the large landowners and also limited their ability to acquire more land. To finance the military, he passed a 30 percent gentry tax on the households of the elite. As a result, money rather than privilege became the means by which anyone could acquire land.

Regardless, the Kangxi Emperor had accomplished something his predecessors hadn't. He had united the Chinese. In the process, though, he did tend to make everyone act uniformly, which may have triggered the revolt in the first place.

A Peaceful Reign

Kangxi was succeeded by the Yongzheng Emperor in 1722. Yongzheng was trained in Confucianism and drew from that to set up an organized hierarchical administration. He also filled his posts with both Han Chinese and Manchu officials. When he viewed the financial situation of the country, he discovered that tax collection was lax. His predecessor had built up debt due to the prolonged revolt, and the treasury was depleting rapidly. The Yongzheng Emperor decided to mount a campaign to enforce the paying of taxes and also did some favors for his most influential supporters. Wisely, he put a lot of money into public improvements like irrigation, education, and the building of public roads.

As a result of this move, a deep financial crisis was avoided. Instead, prosperity was felt among the people. A side effect of this time of peace and prosperity was the growth of the population. China at that time didn't endure a heavy loss of life due to war, and smallpox was no longer a severe threat by the end of the 17th century.

The Fall and Rise of Maritime Trade

In the 16th century, China initiated a policy of isolationism due to piracy and conflicts that ensued because of international relations. Although maritime trade had opened up to some extent, China tended to minimize it. They limited their trading partners and even restricted them from visiting ports. In 1757, most of the legal trade was regulated by the Canton System. This policy restricted trade to Guangzhou (Canton) and a few ports in southern China. Only approved Chinese merchants were allowed to conduct foreign trade, including the British East India Company and the Dutch East India Company, which had been trading with China since the 14th century.

In 1735, the son of the Yongzheng Emperor, who took the name Qianlong Emperor, ascended to the throne. He continued the policy of limited trade with the outside world. In 1793, a British statesman named George Macartney wrote to him regarding opening up another island near Chusan to more trade. The emperor gave him an arrogant response, referring to Europeans as "barbarians," although he may not have intended to be so insulting. "Hitherto, all European nations, including your own barbarian merchants, have carried on trade with our Celestial Empire at Canton." The Qianlong Emperor later remarked in a letter to the king of England, "We possess all things. I place no value on objects strange or ingenious, and I have no use for your country's manufactures."

The Dutch ambassador, **Isaac Titsingh**, fared much better because he meticulously observed protocols and court etiquette when he visited the Qianlong Emperor at his palace.

China's refusal to open a new trading post for Britain impinged upon the British demand for tea, silk, and porcelain, which were demands that had increased exponentially over time. When the English couldn't get those products directly from China, they made arrangements with the Portuguese, who had a long-standing agreement with China to trade at Macao.

The Silver Wedge

Silver, which wasn't mined in China, was a prized commodity. It was used for currency and could be used to tempt the Chinese to trade with other countries. It is estimated that by 1800, China had imported so much silver that it possessed 30 percent of the world's supply of it. Japan was a primary exporter of silver, although political frictions prevented China from getting silver directly from them. Instead, Chinese merchants went to the Portuguese and the Dutch, who acted as intermediaries—for a profit, of course. If Japan didn't export silver, China might have fallen prey to merchants from the Americas or the Spanish colonies. The British and their love of tea drove England to take silver out of their country's treasury in order to get the precious commodity from China.

Population Explosion!

New products from the Americas had been traded with China in exchange for the luxurious silks and porcelain the country was noted for. Two of the most popular products from the Americas were the potato and the peanut. These products helped feed the growing populace of China. By the 18th century, the population of the vast nation numbered close to 300 million people. So much of the country was settled that the number of farms decreased. In addition, fertilization was never a real concern in China. By the time the Jiaqing Emperor assumed the throne in 1796, Manchuria and its environs had the largest amount of arable land.

A return to the discrimination of earlier eras occurred to control population growth and migration into China from other countries. The Han Chinese suffered most from that prejudice and weren't permitted to live in Manchuria, which is just one of many examples of what they had to endure. Many landowners, however, ignored that provision, as these people had the skills to run farms efficiently.

Religious Persecution: The Jahriyya Revolt

Toward the end of the reign of the Qianlong Emperor, there were conflicts and unrest among Muslim residents of the country over issues related to Ramadan and prayer practices. Much of the strife occurred in Qinghai, located in central China. In that area, local governors and judges from the Board of Punishment became involved when different sects of Islam conflicted with one another. Some Muslims became more vocal and complained about the Qing administration, calling the Qing dynasty an infidel regime. In 1781, two subdivisions of a Muslim sect called Sufism—the Jahriyya and the Khafiyya—erupted in violence. There was fighting on the streets and mob violence. The Qing had one of their most famous leaders of the Jahriyya, Ma Mingxin, executed. This only served to accelerate the rebellion. The Qing chose to aid the Khafiyya in the conflict, and subsequently, the Jahriyya Sufis were crushed. Those who were determined to continue to be religious activists were frequently exiled to Xinjiang, Guizhou, and Yunnan to serve as slaves in the military garrisons.

The White Lotus Rebellion of 1794

The name "White Lotus Rebellion" might strike a chord with readers, as an earlier rebellion had occurred during the Yuan dynasty. Although the White Lotus Rebellion of 1794 did bear a marginal resemblance to that earlier revolt, a splinter group from that, called the Wang Lun Uprising, adopted the term on occasion. Like the White Lotus movement of the 14th century, it did have a loose moral tinge to it. The members of the White Lotus Society promised eternal salvation for loyalty to their cause and proclaimed that they adhered to Confucian values.

The Qianlong Emperor and the Jiaqing Emperor both dealt with this rebellion, as it overlapped regimes, and they rejected that idea. The two rulers sought to squash the rebellion and rallied the Green Standard Army.

Local officials and police used this rebellion as a means to extort money from the people for self-protection. There was no proof that they did so, but the practice most likely did happen because of the chaos that permeated the local cities. This revolt lasted about ten years, from 1794 to 1804, and the Qing warriors were successful in eliminating this rebellion. However, there were spin-off groups from this rebellion, including the organizations that sponsored the Eight Trigrams, the Tiger Whips, and the Yihequan ("Boxers").

The Opium Wars

The First Opium War

When the Daoguang Emperor took the throne in 1820, he walked into an ongoing crisis. From the late 1700s, opium had been leaking into China. A maritime network of sea routes was already being used to ship porcelain, tea, and silk to Britain, mostly through third parties. In 1839, the trade with Britain, which was mostly handled in Canton, consisted of porcelain, tea, cotton, and silk. When cotton exports decreased, a trade imbalance occurred. Opium was seen as a replacement for it. Opium is addictive, and the British East India Company took advantage of that. The substance was harvested in Bengal, near India, and it would be purchased by the British, who then would trade it with the Chinese. Many eventually became addicted to the drug and needed it to cope with daily life or else suffer from withdrawals. Chinese smugglers brought it farther inland for distribution to the population, causing the problem to grow worse. Americans competed with the Bengal opium by buying it in Turkey and then offering discounted opium at Indian auctions. Chinese smugglers then bought it, and the British East India Company helped by making illicit agreements to distribute it farther inland. Around

40,000 chests of it were brought into the mainland in 1839 alone. Buyers paid silver for it, so the silver stockpiles in China decreased significantly.

The Daoguang Emperor had made the use of opium illegal and wanted it confiscated at Canton. When shipments of opium poured into Canton, he had his minister, Lin Zexu, blockade the harbor. In response, Britain sent in armed steamships and wiped out thousands of Chinese junks that were sitting in the harbor. The British ships were heavily armed, and so, the Qing forces surrendered. The Treaty of Nanking was signed in 1842, and it was the first of the "unequal treaties" that China was forced to sign. And the term was fairly applied to this treaty. Although the British had to withdraw their troops, the rest of the terms benefited them over the Chinese. The Qing had to repay the British for the opium Lin Zexu confiscated, release all British prisoners, and cede Hong Kong to the British. In addition to Hong Kong, four other ports were opened to the British.: Xiamen, Fuzhou, Ningbo, and Shanghai. The sale of opium, which was the cause of the war in the first place, was not even addressed in the treaty.

However, in China, the use of opium was still illegal. Chinese smugglers continued to distribute opium on the streets to be used at home or in dingy opium dens in secret sub-basements in crowded cities. Authorities were authorized to arrest these people but were generally unsuccessful, mostly due to the fact that local officials were bribed.

The Second Opium War

France complained about the preferential status given to Britain by the Treaty of Nanking and insisted that China open up ports in China for French merchants to use. In 1844, China acquiesced and signed the Treaty of Whampoa. Five ports were opened to them, and as compensation, China was allowed to charge a tariff. The French also used that opportunity to persuade China to permit the presence of Catholic missionaries in China. In 1846, the Daoguang Emperor signed an edict allowing the Chinese to convert to Catholicism if they so wished. Despite that, a French missionary, Father Auguste Chapdelaine, was arrested by a Mandarin bureaucrat for causing unrest and was eventually executed. France was infuriated and sent out ships filled with forces.

Simultaneously, the British had been campaigning for the legalization of opium in China. The opportunity presented itself in 1856 when the Chinese seized a British ship, the *Arrow*, on charges of piracy for the illegal shipment of opium inside China. Ye Mingchen, the Chinese official, arrested the captain and the crew and took possession of the ship, saying that they only did so because the registration had expired.

Soon after this incident, the French allied themselves with Britain, and they attacked Canton. The Second Opium War officially broke out by this point, although it is clear that tensions had been simmering for some time. In 1858, the French and British managed to finally capture Canton. They also captured Ye Mingchen and exiled him to Calcutta, India. The Chinese attacked a US Navy steamer at the mouth of the Peiho River in Tientsin, and the Americans retaliated by attacking and capturing Chinese forts on the Pearl River. The Xianfeng Emperor was, at the time, embroiled in the Taiping Rebellion (see below), and his resources were becoming thin. He was forced to succumb to Western pressures and sought peace.

In 1858, the British and the French asked America and Russia to join them in drawing up the Treaty of Tientsin, which was another one of the "unequal treaties" in the eyes of the Chinese. This treaty granted foreign countries the right to use ten more ports in China to conduct trade, all foreign ships were permitted to sail on the Yangtze River, and foreign merchants were allowed to travel inside China. It also allowed Christian missionaries to spread their message across China peacefully, and perhaps worse of all, it legalized the import of opium. By the time the treaty was finalized in 1860, between 50,000 to 60,000 chests were entering the country every year.

Russia and China had border disputes in the prior century, but in 1858, China negotiated an ancillary treaty, the Treaty of Aigun, because they couldn't afford to start another conflict. By virtue of that treaty, China agreed to move the Russia-China border southward in order to give them access to a "warm water" port. That was important for Russia, as it would then be able to ship goods out even in the winter.

The Taiping Rebellion

Zeng Guofan, a military general, became a hero in the Taiping Rebellion of 1850–1864. It erupted when a deluded man by the name of Hong Xiuquan preached that he was the brother of Jesus Christ. Hong was a self-styled Christian with his own version of Christianity. He called his organization the Taiping Heavenly Kingdom. Hong had not only religious ideals but also very opinionated political views. However, he told his followers that they were fighting a "holy war." Hong's interest, however, was spurred by economic interests and power. That led him to command the lands in southern China below the Yangtze River. Despite the fact that Christianity doesn't promote violence, the Taiping Rebellion was one of the bloodiest in Chinese history. Boldly, Hong and his troops tried to annex Beijing but failed due to the efforts of Zeng Guofan.

When Hong Xiuquan died in 1864, his movement died with him. However, the contemporaries of that time remember that he was responsible for the deaths of ten to twenty million, including both troops and civilians.

The Great Qing Legal Code

During the Qing dynasty, the legal code contained hundreds of statutes, and many were applied during the religious persecutions. China had laws regulating government personnel, revenue, civil and religious rites, marriage, military affairs, homicide, and even construction. Offenses weren't split into civil or criminal as in other countries. Confucianism espoused an inextricable relationship between business and morals. Therefore, there was no civil code that didn't have a criminal component. Corporal punishment and even torture were among the penalties rendered if a party was found guilty. A confession was always perceived as an offense that merited punishment. Most people who filed charges over civil matters tended to settle their issues out of court, so the threat of harsh physical punishment acted as a prime motivator for conflict resolution. There were very harsh penalties for homosexuality, and adultery was strictly forbidden. Even widows had a difficult time remarrying, even though that would have been legal under the law, as the women couldn't prove they hadn't committed adultery. Many remained celibate, and some even committed suicide since they were unable to support themselves and their children. The Great Qing Legal Code lasted until the overthrow of the Qing dynasty.

Self-Strengthening

Zeng Guofan, like many of his Chinese compatriots, was humiliated by the country's defeats to the Western powers during the Opium Wars. Opium wasn't the issue; the issue was the fact that China didn't have enough military strength to be able to command respect and make demands of other counties in international crises.

In 1860, the British and the French had worked their way into Beijing, and China had little control over the unbridled freedoms these foreign powers were taking. Even the Christians, who had been granted the right to proselytize in 1846, were dodging tax obligations they had agreed to observe. While the Treaty of Tientsin was being finalized in 1860, the British and French were forcing China to accept more and more concessions by attacking the emperor's summer palaces. Zeng Guofan worked with noted Chinese statesman Li Hongzhang to manufacture more powerful weapons and put China on an equal military basis with the Western countries.

Li was instrumental in the attempts to upgrade China, setting up the China Merchants Steam Navigation Company in 1872, the coal mines in Kaiping in 1877, a telegraph network in 1879, and two factories that manufactured cotton in 1890.

Many of the more conservative and studious Chinese preferred to return to the past and secretly wished that the West would "go away." Li's and Zheng's efforts were heroic, as they had to convince Chinese authorities that the country needed to be nationalized. China needed to be united as a country and eschew factional conflicts, as they would only serve to weaken the country from within.

The Emigration Phenomenon

The population of China had increased substantially during the late 19th century, and the drain on resources was extreme. Female infanticide was on the rise, as there were very few opportunities for women to become wage-earners. Even young men couldn't find profitable work in China, and many emigrated to other countries. They went to Australia, America, Malaysia, Malacca, Borneo, the South Pacific islands, and Southeast Asian countries. In some Buddhist countries, like Thailand and Vietnam, the Chinese intermarried and virtually disappeared as a distinct culture. In Muslim countries like Java or in Christian countries like the Philippines, they lived in separate communities.

Unfortunately, many of these emigrants were hired by unscrupulous foreign employers and worked for very low wages. They were called "coolies," from the Chinese word *kuli*, meaning "bitter laborer." They were basically indentured servants who didn't earn enough to advance their lives forward in any way. In the American West, many were hired by railroad companies and treated very badly.

Preamble to War

In 1876, Korea and Japan signed a treaty, opening up trade between the two countries. Huang Zunxian, the Chinese ambassador to Korea, recommended that Korea maintain friendly relations with Japan. He felt that Japan would counterbalance any undesirable influence by Russia. At that time, Japan wasn't seen as a threat to the power of China.

Japan was also interested in a cordial relationship with the US to further balance any possible threat from Russia. However, when the Americans established relations with Korea, they overlooked the fact that Korea had a history of being a tributary state of China, which started back in 1637. The US felt that Korea should be considered an independent state. The skilled statesman Li Hongzhang was in charge of the Chinese-Korean policy and presented a compromise that would satisfy both the US and China. So, the Japan-Korea Treaty was amended to state that Korea was "an independent state enjoying the same sovereign rights as does Japan."

Li Hongzhang spoke with Korean representatives and recommended that they emulate the "self-strengthening" policy that China had started and introduce reforms that would help them relate to other countries from a position of strength—not overwhelming strength but at least equal strength. The Chinese then sent over a military unit to train Korean soldiers in warfare techniques and provided them with upgraded weapons.

The Japanese were ambivalent about Korea's interest in reform. Some were very much in favor of it and wanted to participate in helping Korea develop, but other Japanese preferred that Koreans focus on these improvements by themselves and thus be more passive on the world stage. Regardless of the differences of opinion in Japan, the Korean Prince Regent Heungseon Daewongun saw to it that reform efforts were started.

The Meddling Starts

Korea's relationships with China and Japan were tested in 1882 when a riot broke out in Korea during a drought. It started in Imo but inexplicably spread to the Japanese legation in Korea. Six Japanese were killed, and riots broke out throughout the city.

Japan then deployed four warships to Korea, and China sent in 4,500 troops. The two countries were now competing for control over Korean affairs. As a result of the Imo Incident, Korea made reparations and penalized the chief perpetrators of the rebellion, which had resulted in the deaths of Japanese representatives. When the Koreans blamed Heungseon Daewongun for the riot, the Chinese interfered by taking him to China, where he was confined.

Korea became a prize to be won or a pawn to be used. China wanted the Korean reforms to move along gradually, while Japan wanted them to make rapid improvements.

The Japanese dispatched a fleet into the Korean harbors of Pusan and Chempulpo, but they assured Li Hongzhang that they had no intention of attacking. They indicated that they simply wanted to balance off the Chinese forces already in the country.

King GoJong of Korea insisted that the Japanese depart. However, Japan adamantly refused.

The First Sino-Japanese War

In 1894, Japan and China reached a pivotal moment having to do with the nature of their relations with Korea. Emperor Meiji of Japan said, "Korea is an independent state. She was first introduced into the family of nations by the advice and guidance of Japan. It has, however, been China's habit to designate Korea as her dependency." The Guangxu Emperor of China retorted, "Korea has been our tributary for the past two hundred odd years. She has given us tribute all this time, which is a matter known to the world. For the past dozen years or so Korea has been troubled by repeated insurrections and we, in sympathy with our small tributary, have repeatedly sent her aid."

The First Sino-Japanese War was very short, lasting a little over eight months. Despite the fact that they had revitalized their military, China wasn't ready. In July, the Japanese vessels *Naniwa*, *Akitsushima,* and *Yoshino* captured and sunk the *Kowshing*, a British transport ship subcontracted by China to carry members of the Green Standard Army and Eight Banners Army into Asan, Korea.

The Japanese heavily outnumbered the Chinese, and at the Battle of Seonghwan, they defeated the Chinese, placing them within fifty miles of Seoul. The bulk of the Chinese shored up their defenses in northern Korea, sensing that the Japanese would make a strike there.

More Chinese were stationed in northern Korea than at the prior battle near Asan. Most were guarding the capital city of Pyongyang. The Japanese separated their forces into three divisions. Two engaged the Chinese at opposing diagonal corners of the city walls, and the third division attacked from the rear. After the Japanese won this battle, the Chinese pulled out of the north and withdrew toward the mouth of the Yalu River, which feeds out of the Yellow Sea, near the Chinese/Korean border.

At the Battle of the Yalu River, which took place in 1894, the Japanese navy's frontal formations proved to be superior to those of the Chinese. Although the Japanese made a number of tactical errors, the Chinese used an ineffective wedge formation, inviting broadside attacks. At the end of this one-day battle, China's Beiyang fleet withdrew.

The Chinese troops then moved to defend their own homeland in Manchuria when they saw the Japanese were moving toward their shores. However, the Japanese were able to capture the Chinese outpost of Hushan before moving on land to capture six towns in Manchuria.

In Port Arthur, the Japanese reported that they saw the decapitated head of a dead Japanese soldier on display. They retaliated with an indiscriminate massacre of thousands of Chinese soldiers and civilians. A Japanese eyewitness reported, "Anyone we saw in the town, we killed. The streets were filled with corpses...Blood was flowing and the smell was awful." The estimates of the number killed differ vastly. Some reported 1,000 were killed, while other media sources reported as many as 60,000 were slaughtered. Some have conjectured that the larger number was exaggerated by journalists for political reasons.

In the city of Weihaiwei in northeast China, Chinese soldiers stayed behind the fortification walls when the Japanese placed the city under siege. The Chinese abandoned the fort in the bitter cold of January 1895, and the battle moved to the Yellow Sea. After winning the Battle of Weihaiwei, the Japanese took over the Liaodong Peninsula, which borders northwestern Korea.

The ground forces of both parties were engaged in Manchuria and its environs, and the Japanese conquered six cities there. They then headed toward the Manchurian capital, Mukden. The Japanese captured the town of Haicheng on the Liaodong Peninsula. The Chinese made four attempts to retake the city but failed every time. As they were anxious to end the war, the Japanese decided they wanted to take either Mukden or Beijing, as losing either one would greatly cripple the Chinese forces.

The Japanese then surprised China and the international observers by capturing the Pescadores Islands in the Taiwan Strait. The Japanese wanted control of the Pescadores because that would be their key to gaining control of Taiwan. Those islands could have been used by Japan to prevent the arrival of Chinese reinforcements to Taiwan, as well as open the gates to gain Taiwan in a subsequent treaty.

Their strategy worked.

The Treaty of Shimonoseki

By virtue of the Shimonoseki Treaty, which was signed in April of 1895, Japan and China recognized the independence of Korea. Japan received Taiwan, the Pescadores Islands, and the Liaodong Peninsula "in perpetuity." The Japanese were also permitted to conduct trade on the Yangtze River.

The Qing Empire was humiliated. They had to pay 13,600 tons of silver in war reparations, and the Chinese inhabitants in Korea were forced to leave. Chinese settlers in Taiwan and the Taiwanese fought a guerilla-style rebellion against the Japanese. Many were slaughtered. Women were raped, and peasants were thrown off their lands unless they stayed on as tenant farmers.

Too Little, Too Late

In 1898, a brilliant politician and philosopher, Kang Youwei, obtained an audience with the Guangxu Emperor. He had a great deal of foresight and tried to encourage China to reform its antique approach to government. Even the Empress Dowager Cixi, who effectively ruled China from 1861 to 1908, was interested in his proposals. Some of them were:

    1. Elimination of the civil service examinations, which only served to separate the applicants into the elites and the commoners

    2. Education in Western liberal arts

    3. Education of the imperial family abroad

4. Establishment of a constitutional monarchy

5. Introduction of some elements of capitalism to motivate people to work harder

6. Industrialization

7. Restructuring of the military

8. Construction of a railway system

These proposals were a part of the Hundred Days' Reform, a movement that the Guangxu Emperor promoted along with like-minded followers. However, too many people, including Empress Dowager Cixi, were consumed by dreams of the distant past and had difficulty accepting those propositions.

The Boxer Rebellion

Wrapped up in the nostalgia of the days when China was an isolationist country, a group of well-meaning but naïve young men trained in the martial arts felt that foreigners and missionaries needed to be expelled—all of them. So, in 1899, they started randomly killing foreigners and missionaries in Beijing and Tientsin.

The Dowager Empress Cixi sided with the Boxers. She complained, "The foreigners had been aggressive toward us, infringed on our territorial integrity, and trampled our people under their feet." The Boxers placed foreign legations and missions in Beijing and Tientsin under siege. However, 20,000 troops from other nations soon marched on Tientsin and Beijing, lifted the siege, and even looted the cities. The empress dowager and the emperor, who were hiding in the Forbidden City, fled.

Li Hongzhang was called upon to negotiate, but there was little he could do. He had warned China of the need to modernize, but China had been much too slow to respond to his call for action. By way of reparations, China had to pay 450 million ounces of silver; fortunately, Li was able to get his opponents to agree to an installment plan.

Beginning of the End

When the Empress Dowager Cixi was in her seventies, she announced that Puyi, the grandson of the emperor, would assume the throne after Emperor Guangxu. When the court heard that, they took two-year-old Puyi to see the empress. This was a traumatic event for him, and he once wrote about the meeting, saying, "I remember suddenly finding myself surrounded by strangers, while before me was hung a drab curtain through which I could see an emaciated and terrifyingly hideous face. This was Cixi."

The Guangxu Emperor died in 1908 "under mysterious circumstances." He was only 37 years old. A day later, Dowager Empress Cixi died. Many believe that Cixi, knowing the end was near, had the emperor poisoned. In 2008, a test was done on the body of the Guangxu Emperor, which found that his remains contained 2,000 times the normal amount of arsenic in a person's body. This leads historians to speculate that Cixi had the emperor killed so he could not continue advancing his progressive reforms.

Now, the throne of the Qing dynasty, which could never really break out of the shell of its isolationist fantasies, was now in the hands of a child, a child who was frightened by the face of an old woman. And while his father, Prince Chun, would become regent to the young boy, Puyi would grow up knowing nothing other than the fact that he was the emperor of China.

Chapter 9 – Revolutionary Madness

Wuchang Uprising

Toward the end of the Qing dynasty, some of the newly proposed administrative and national reforms were underway. One of them was the reorganization of the Chinese army, then called the Beiyang Army. It was mobilized to suppress violent resistors of the proposed railroad system. In 1910, the Qing dynasty made arrangements with a Western finance company to initiate the project. However, the diehard conservatives like the Boxers rejected these "capitalists." The man in charge of the project, Sheng Xuanhuai, nationalized the endeavor. Massive rallies and strikes took place, mostly in Chengdu.

This phase of the uprising was propelled by underground revolutionary groups such as the Tongmenghui, which was formed from several factions, including the Revive China Society. The Furen Literary Society and the Progressive Association supported them. The Tongmenghui was being funded by the wealthy Sun family, who owned thousands of acres in Hawaii.

Sun Yat-sen, who greatly promoted the cause of the Tongmenghui, believed in a revolutionary philosophy and raised money from many countries in order to sponsor some of the uprisings in China. When his intentions became known, he was essentially exiled, and he lived in a number of countries, including the United States, Canada, Great Britain, and Japan. When he heard about the Wuchang Uprising of 1911, Sun returned to China.

These groups were in the process of making explosive devices to be used for a large-scale revolution. When a supervisor named Sun Wu was injured while the explosives were being assembled, word leaked out about these rebel factions. Three of them were executed, but 5,000 dissidents escaped the Qing authorities.

Nearly one-third of the Qing defectors were military members, and they soon mutinied. In 1911, the army traitors attacked the garrison at Huguang, seizing the local Qing viceroy in the process.

The rebel commander, Xiong Bingkun, gathered together all the revolutionary forces he could and prepared to attack the Qing forces with 100,000 men. The highly motivated revolutionaries, composed of revolutionary cells and ex-military soldiers, conquered Wuchang.

The loyal members of the Beiyang Army under Yuan Shikai were called upon to suppress the rebellion. In the Battle of Yangxia, which took place between October and the beginning of December, fighting broke out at the cities of Hankou and Hanyang along the Yangtze River. However, the revolutionaries had inferior weapons and lost the battle at Hankou. The Beiyang Army then decided to burn the city. At Hanyang, there was fighting throughout the streets, even in houses. The Qing army took possession of the munitions factory and destroyed the rebels' artillery. As many as 3,000 revolutionaries died there. Despite those setbacks, many other provinces defected, including Sichuan, Nanjing, and Shaanxi. In addition, the entire Qing navy defected.

The Xinhai Revolution of 1911

The Wuchang Uprising kicked off what is known as the Xinhai Revolution. Sun Yat-sen, who would become the leader of the revolution, was still in the United States fundraising when this chaotic outbreak occurred. He wasn't aware of this revolt until months later, after which he went to England and contacted other Western countries in order to assure their neutrality and receive financing for a new republic. After this attempt, which proved unsuccessful, Sun Yat-sen returned to China, arriving there in late December 1911. However, when Sun Sat-yen was abroad, the Xinhai Revolution was in search of a leader. The people thrust the role upon Li Yuanhong, a military commander.

Thus, this revolution was truly "home-grown." Many dissident provinces staged their own attacks:

The Changsha Restoration, October 22nd

The Shaanxi Uprising, October 22nd

The Jiujiang Uprising, October 23rd

The Shanxi Taiyuan Revolt, October 29th

The Kunming "Double Ninth" Uprising, October 30th, so-named because it was the ninth day of the ninth month in the old Chinese calendar

The Nanchang Uprising, October 31st

The Shanghai Armed Uprising, November 3rd

The Guizhou Uprising, November 4th

The Zhejiang Uprising, November 4th

The Jiangsu Restoration, November 5th

The Anhui Uprising, November 5th

The Guangxi Uprising, November 7th

The Guangdong Independence, November 9th

The Fujian Independence, November 11th

The Shandong Independence, November 13th

The Ningxia Uprising, November 17th

The Sichuan Independence, November 21st

The Nanjing Uprising, December 3rd

There were two regions that deviated from this revolutionary pattern: Tibet and Mongolia. Their status was held in abeyance until order returned.

Last-Ditch Qing

The rebels, who were mostly from the military, took over Beijing. In a fit of desperation, the Qing dynasty proposed a constitutional monarchy with General Yuan Shikai as its new prime minister. The child emperor's adoptive mother, Empress Dowager Longyu, proposed that the emperor and his family assume only a ceremonial role.

However, when Sun Yat-sen arrived back in China in late December 1911, he was immediately appointed provisional president of the newly formed government, which was set up in Nanjing.

Yuan and Sun then negotiated a solution. Yuan Shikai would be the first president of the Republic of China, and the Qing emperor, Puyi, would officially abdicate with the understanding that the imperial family could continue to live in the Forbidden City.

Chapter 10 – The Republic of China to the People's Republic of China

The days of the dynasties were now over. General Yuan Shikai was inaugurated as the provisional president of the Republic of China in March 1912. He and his confidantes then moved to Beijing, and the new government received international recognition.

Financial Entanglements

Upon the launch of the new administration, China was in a financial crisis due to the expenditures of the many revolts. Yuan Shikai took out a number of loans from foreign parties. Although the investments were risky, foreign financial institutions extended loans to China. To protect themselves from financial risk, though, the investors charged an extremely high interest rate. The amount borrowed amounted to 21 million pounds of silver. Within three years, the government ran an annual deficit of two million pounds of silver.

Administration

In March, a proposed constitution was drafted, and arrangements were made for public voting. Only 10 percent of the male population were permitted to vote. Those who were bankrupt or addicted opium-smokers were excluded, along with women.

Sun Yat-sen, the initial leader of the revolutionaries, organized his own political party called the Kuomintang (KMT) after the Xinhai Revolution of 1911. Another party was created in 1912, the Republican Party, to which Yuan Shikai belonged. This party was a bit more conservative in nature compared to the KMT. In December 1912, an election was held, and Song Jiaoren was instrumental in ensuring victories for his party, the Kuomintang. It was widely thought that Song would become the next prime minister. However, tragedy struck.

In March 1913, as Song traveled to the railroad station to report to Beijing, a man approached him and shot him. Song died two days later. A commission investigated the assassination, but one by one, those thought to be involved were murdered. Due to the lack of evidence, Yuan Shikai, who most likely orchestrated the assassination, was never charged with anything.

It is thought that Yuan did this because of the popularity of Song and the KMT. In order to secure the support of those in Parliament, Yuan had regularly bribed them. Those who refused the bribes were dismissed. He also had the support of those who were still loyal in the Beiyang Army.

Second Revolution

In the summer of 1913, seven southern provinces rebelled because they felt that Yuan Shikai was responsible for the assassination of Song Jiaoren and because they felt he obtained his position through political manipulation rather than merit. In addition, the armies hadn't been paid. Members of Sun Yat-sen's Kuomintang participated but were defeated by Yuan's superior military strength under General Zhang Xun. Yuan then dissolved the parliament and appointed his own cabinet, which made him a president with dictatorial powers. His vice president was Li Yuanhong.

This wasn't Sun Yat-sen's vision for a new China. Sun attempted to rebuild opposition against Yuan and formed the Chinese

Revolutionary Party. By this time, the Republican Party had been merged, along with other like-minded parties, into the Progressive Party. Although they supported Yuan in the Second Revolution, they didn't support his move to disband the KMT. They, like the Revolutionary Party, wanted to remove Yuan from power.

World War I

In 1914, World War I broke out. China declared its neutrality right from the beginning. However, there was some consternation over the fact that a German colony had been established in Shandong province back in 1897. Japan wanted the Germans out of there, and the Japanese used this as a wedge to involve China in the war. Yuan was in favor of expelling the Germans too, and despite China's declared neutrality, Yuan Shikai agreed to put 50,000 troops under Britain's control, provided they expelled the Germans in Shandong. Britain turned down that proposal.

Knowing that China didn't have a strong military force of its own, Japan simply annexed Shandong and ousted the Germans. Japan then sent China the Twenty-One Demands in 1915, which included granting Japan economic control of the railways in the north and give them long-term offices in Shandong, Manchuria, and Fujian. Yuan accepted those demands with some modifications. The Chinese population was livid.

After this, the Chinese joined the Allied side and mostly escorted troop transports and supply ships for the Allies in the Mediterranean.

To control the public opposition to his acceptance of the Twenty-One Demands, Yuan coerced journalists and writers to support him in their editorials and articles.

However, in 1916, he proclaimed himself the Hongxian Emperor and wanted to re-establish the monarchy. Provinces erupted in riots and rebellions. His governor Cal E and Tang Yiyao, governor of the influential Yunnan province, created the National Protection War. Many districts declared themselves independent of the emperor. The Beiyang Army was sent in to quell the rebellions, but lacked little motivation, as they haven't been paid in quite some time.

Yuan Shikai didn't suspect that reaction, and his rule as emperor only lasted 83 days, after which he ruled as president. When he died of a kidney condition in 1916, Vice President Li Yuanhong took over the government.

The Warlords and a "Coup"

Li Yuanhong and Parliament ruled in a vacuum. They had virtually little control over the whole country. In 1916, the petty leaders of the various provinces assumed control of their own "mini-kingdoms." They had no political parties to support them, however.

In 1917, Li Yuanhong's field marshal, Zhang Xun, rose up and announced a preposterous measure—the reinstatement of the former emperor, Puyi! He was now eleven years old. On July 1ˢᵗ, Puyi was set up in Beijing with a court and his handlers; however, he only ruled for eleven days. Soon after this, feuding warlords took over the city. Some were intelligent men, while others were just glorified bandits. Three of the strongest warlords were Zhang Zuolin, Wu Peifu, and Feng Yuxiang. Loyalty meant little to most of them. Feng, for example, once fought under Wu Peifu but then split from him to form his own group. There was constant pillaging of farms and shops, along with indiscriminate slaughter. Although the warlords only oversaw local areas, the chaos they produced threatened to continue for years to come.

One of the most troubling of the warlord groups was the Beiyang Army, which consisted of the loyal followers of the Qing dynasty. After the dynasty had collapsed, the Beiyang remained a threat because they were experienced and well-organized.

Rebirth of Unification Efforts

At the end of World War I, according to the Treaty of Versailles, Japan was allowed to keep the concessions they had in those regions, which the Chinese found astonishing. Sun Yat-sen collaborated with the southern provinces and resurrected the Kuomintang in 1917. He served as a "president" and again tried to get funds and the support of the Western countries. That attempt failed, so Sun sought Soviet support for the reunification efforts. Mikhail Borodin, an agent for the

Comintern (Communist International), an organization promoting world communism, conferred with Sun Yat-sen in 1923. Together, they created the First United Front.

The First United Front was an alliance between the Kuomintang (KMT) and the Communist Party of China (CPC). The CPC had been founded in 1921 and was quickly growing in popularity. Chiang Kai-shek, Sun's lieutenant in the Kuomintang, and Sun Yat-sen didn't want to create a communist state. While Chiang Kai-shek had studied the Soviet system and admired its organizational aspects, he disagreed with the communist principles it promoted. Sun Yat-sen's vision was to develop a reunified China according to three phases: 1) reunion of China by force, 2) politically-based education in the new government, and 3) introduction of democracy.

In 1925, Sun died, and Chiang Kai-shek took over the reins. He created a military arm to support the Kuomintang, the National Revolutionary Army.

The Nanjing Decade

In 1926, Chiang Kai-shek launched the Northern Expedition. The purpose of this was to eliminate the threats from the rival Beiyang Army and warlords like Zhang Zuolin, Wu Peifu, and Feng Yuxiang. Under his leadership, the army wiped out the warlords and succeeded in controlling half of China.

In 1927, Chiang Kai-shek seized control of Nanjing from the local warlord, Sun Chuanfang. A problem arose when Chiang discovered that a heavily communist faction led by Wang Jingwei was set up in Wuhan province. That government, following orders from Soviet liaison Mikhail Borodin, tried futilely to strip Chiang of his powers. Wang met Chiang in Shanghai to discuss a power-sharing agreement. Wang indicated he would consider it and returned to Wuhan. However, the government in Wuhan rejected the compromise and prepared to go to Shanghai, where Chiang Kai-shek was currently seated.

In April 1927, the National Revolutionary Army reached Shanghai. Shanghai had a large majority of Communists, and Chiang was determined to rid China from Soviet influence. Chiang and his men tore through the city, arrested and executed known members of the Communist Party, and purged the government of them. As many as 12,000 people were killed. This event is known as the Shanghai massacre. Chiang didn't stop there, however. He initiated a large-scale massacre throughout all of China, known as the White Terror. Over 300,000 people were killed, and blood ran thick in the streets. The Communists who were still left in China mostly moved into rural districts where the Kuomintang wasn't present.

Chiang then worked to convince the provincial leaders to give up their independent local governments and turn them over to a central government. After hearing about the cruelty of Chiang's forces, the people were afraid and conformed.

Although total unification wasn't achieved, the country was divided into five realms: Nanjing, Guangxi, the Guominjun, another sector controlled by Yan Xishan, and the semi-autonomous state of Manchuria led by Zhang Xueliang.

Chiang Kai-shek then moved the Kuomintang government from Beijing to Nanjing and kept it there for ten years, which is why it was called the "Nanjing decade."

Modernization

Diplomatic efforts to build relations with the rest of the world were developed and continued after the Nanjing decade. Banking reforms were established, and public health facilities were upgraded and created. The legal and penal system was brought up to the standards exercised by other countries. In addition to these efforts, legislation against narcotics use and distribution were passed and enforced, and the manufacturing of agricultural machinery was increased.

While some characterize Chiang Kai-shek as a capitalist, he eschewed capitalism nearly as much as he did communism. He severely criticized the "imperialists," forbidding them from holding any governmental positions and coercing them into donating large portions of their money to the country, especially for modernization.

After all, neighboring countries had modernized—Japan, in particular. In fact, China made a business deal with Japan to build and manage the South Manchuria Railroad. It was a prosperous arrangement for both countries. However, in September of 1931, there was an explosion at the railroad. Japanese soldiers who were protecting the railway line at Mukden blamed the Chinese for causing it. They rushed over to a Chinese garrison nearby and attacked it. Hostilities accelerated, and a battle broke out in 1931. This event was called the Mukden Incident. This led to the invasion of Manchuria and the setting up of a puppet state there.

Mukden Incident of 1931

Chiang Kai-shek became alarmed about the conflict and appealed to the League of Nations, an international body that was intended to mediate such crises and stop pending wars. The League agreed with China and asked Japan to return Manchuria. Japan didn't agree with this ruling and left the League.

At that time, Chiang was in north-central China in the city of Xi'an with his National Revolutionary Army, and they were in the process of expelling the Communists. Chiang Kai-shek met with two of his generals, Yang Hucheng and Zhang Xueliang. Both men wanted Chiang to cease his hostilities against the Chinese Communists and had the great Chiang Kai-shek arrested. This was an outrageous act of betrayal.

Madame Chiang Kai-shek Intercedes

Chiang's wife, Soong May-ling, was politically astute and often advised her husband upon Chinese affairs. After hearing of Chiang's kidnapping in Xi'an, she advised him to shift his focus away from his obsession with the elimination of the Communist Party of China and turn his attention to the very serious Japanese threat. During negotiations with his captors, she advised Chiang to accept their terms, which were the cessation of hostilities between the Chinese Communists and to unite the Communist troops with the National Revolutionary Army forces in order to expel Japan from Manchuria and China. Once he agreed to those terms, Chiang was released, and he joined up with the Communist leader, Zhou Enlai.

In 1937, the Marco Polo Bridge Incident occurred. The Japanese, who were missing a soldier after a training exercise, demanded entry into a Chinese garrison to search for him. When the Chinese refused this, the Japanese attempted to force their way in, and tensions escalated until conflict broke out. Many consider this to be the start of the Second Sino-Japanese War, and some even consider it to be the starting date for World War II.

The Second Sino-Japanese War

Because Japan had been helping China upgrade its industrial base, it was well aware of the fact that China was behind other countries in terms of modernization. That made China very vulnerable. Japan craved the resources and opportunities China held so they could expand their own sphere of influence in the Pacific region. The Mukden Incident had presented them with a golden opportunity, as the Japanese could use Manchuria as a base in order to take over China.

This was a tenuous union, but one that was needed because Japan was their mutual enemy and a great threat to China. This merger of the Communist and Nationalist forces was called the Second United Front.

The Battle of Shanghai, August 13th–November 26th, 1937

This was the first major battle of the Second Sino-Japanese War. At first, Chiang's forces conducted an air war with Japan over the city. However, Japan's Mitsubishi A5M aircraft were far more superior than China's Curtiss F11C biplanes and shot them out of the sky. It eventually turned into a ground war in the city. The Chinese ground forces of 70,000 far outnumbered the Japanese troops of 6,300 marines, so their prospects for victory looked good. Shortly afterward, Japan sent in as many as 100,000 of their Imperial forces. As a result, the Chinese army was forced to retreat, leaving Shanghai in the hands of the Japanese.

The Capture of Nanjing (Nanking), December 1ˢᵗ-13ᵗʰ, 1937

In 1937, the Japanese captured Nanjing. While there, they killed not only soldiers but Chinese civilians. This event, known as the Nanking massacre, saw between 40,000 to 300,000 deaths. The sources conflict greatly on the actual number, as people debate on the geographical boundary of the massacre as well as the timespan of it. Some Japanese claim only several hundred died, and a small minority believe that the massacre never took place at all. In addition to the murder of innocents, widespread looting and raping occurred. Civilians fled to safety zones by the thousands, and China essentially lost control of the city of Nanjing.

The Battle of Taierzhuang, March 24ᵗʰ-April 7ᵗʰ

The Japanese army had a tendency to take matters into their own hands, and they often avoided getting permission from the Japanese government to continue the war. So, they marched into Jiangsu. The Chinese resistance was strong, and in April of 1938, the Chinese confronted the Japanese at Taierzhuang, which was located on the Grand Canal. Much to the surprise of the headstrong Japanese troops, they were beaten, making this battle the first major Chinese victory of the war.

The Japanese countered by attacking and capturing Kaifeng, the capital of Henan province, and threatened to take Zhengzhou as well. Chiang Kai-shek and his men knew the area well and understood its tendency to flood. In order to stop the Japanese rampage, the Chinese broke down some of the dikes on the Yellow River. Water gushed upon the Japanese troops, and Japanese soldiers died by the thousands. Chinese civilians reported that the rivers and streams were loaded with rotting corpses. Death and its insipid odor were everywhere.

Japan called for negotiations in order to stop the bloodshed, but Chiang Kai-shek delayed. The Japanese then launched attacks at Suixian-Zaoyang, Changsha, and South Guangxi. Messages running through Japan's line of communication had been delayed because of the immense amount of territory Japan was trying to control simultaneously. Therefore, they lost each battle.

The United States opposed this large-scale invasion of China, so they started sending supplies and money for China to support the war effort. With the Japanese attack on Pearl Harbor in December 1941, the Second Sino-Japanese War quickly merged into another conflict of World War II, opening up the Pacific theater of the war.

China in World War II

The United States declared war against Japan after the attack on its naval base, and China soon joined them. At the Battle of Changsha, which started on December 24th, 1941, the Chinese assisted the British forces in Hong Kong. The Japanese fended off the Chinese army and entered Changsha. However, they hadn't planned on China's next actions, as the Chinese forces outside of the city completely surrounded the Japanese in Changsha. After suffering heavy casualties, the Japanese withdrew on January 15th.

In 1942, in Burma, the British were surrounded by the Japanese at the town of Yenangyaung but were rescued by the large 38th Corps of the Chinese army. The Japanese swooped into Zhejiang and Jiangxi provinces, but they were forced out by the Chinese army. In Burma, Chiang Kai-shek worked alongside Lieutenant Joseph Stillwell of the United States to break a Japanese blockade. Chiang and Stillwell disagreed over tactics, as Chiang suspected that Stillwell wanted to use the Chinese to help protect the British territories rather than bring Allied forces into China to expel the Japanese. America decided to replace Stillwell with General Albert Coady Wedemeyer, who was more willing to cooperate.

In 1944, Chinese troops came in from India, and with others from Yunnan province, they attacked the Japanese in Burma, freeing up a critical supply route into China. In 1945, the Chinese successfully retook Hunan and Guangxi. The Soviets, who were on the Allied side, invaded the Japanese in Manchuria and freed it, giving it back to the Chinese. General Wedemeyer and the Chinese planned to retake

Guangdong province and readied their forces to do so. However, the bombings of Nagasaki and Hiroshima put a sudden stop to the war.

The Japanese troops in China formally surrendered to Chiang Kai-shek on September 9th, 1945, at 9:00 a.m. This was the ninth day of the ninth month at the ninth hour. 9-9-9 was significant to the Chinese, as the number nine stood for "long-lasting." At the end of the war, China was regarded as a great power.

The Deadly Aftermath

The estimates of the Chinese killed or wounded in the Second Sino-Japanese War and World War II are staggering. Between fifteen and twenty million died, and fifteen million were wounded. There were about 95 million refugees. Many of them were from Guangdong province, as there wasn't anywhere for the inhabitants to resettle because of the widespread devastation. About $383 million was spent on the war effort.

The Two Chinas

The Second United Front in China, which had fought against Japan, was a precarious union between Chiang Kai-shek's Nationalists and the Chinese Communist Party. There was a tacit agreement that these two opposing political groups would suspend their differences during the course of the two wars, but as soon as World War II came to a conclusion, the tensions between the two arose once more.

Chiang Kai-shek had always had strenuous objections to the inclusion of communism in China, but he wanted some kind of peace after the fighting had stopped. So, he contacted Mao Zedong, the chairman of the Chinese Communist Party, as he was desirous of reaching a compromise. Chiang Kai-shek, Mao Zedong, and American ambassador Patrick Hurley conferred together. However, as soon as they held the initial private conference, conflicts broke out between the Communists and the Nationalists. Both walked away from the negotiations.

The US decided to send in George Marshall in December 1945 to coax the two groups to return to the negotiating table. They agreed to reorganize the government, convoke a national assembly, adopt a constitution, and make reforms in the areas of economics and the structure of military forces.

The meeting, as it turned out, was merely theoretical but not practical. In Manchuria, where the Japanese were still withdrawing after the war, there was a scramble for power. Nationalist troops rushed into Mukden, and Communist soldiers solidified positions in northern Manchuria. The fighting spread to Hebei, Jiangsu, Shantung, and Chengde. After Nationalist troops took over the city of Kalgan, the Nationalists set up the first meeting of a national assembly, without notifying Zhou Enlai. The assembly then proceeded to draft a constitution, without input from the Chinese Communist Party. Zhou was enraged, and George Marshall condemned the Nationalists for making this foolish move and left China.

One of Chiang Kai-shek's ministers, General Zhang Zhizhong, contacted the Communists and expressed a willingness to resume talks. He restated the initial conditions discussed at the beginning of the negotiations, but the Communists were no longer interested.

The Communists then took over the railroad in Mukden that led to central China. Mao announced, "The Chinese People's Liberation Army has carried the fight into the Kuomintang area. This is a turning point in history."

By 1947, the Nationalist forces had lost much of its military strength. They concentrated their efforts on Manchuria, but due to their military inferiority, they became a defensive rather than an offensive force. Under General Lin Biao, the Communist troops sought to strike weakened positions along the Nationalist lines and hammered away at them. The strategy worked well, and the Communists regained control of Manchuria in 1948. They then moved to other northern provinces and later regained control of Shantung, Yunnan, and Zhengzhou from the Nationalists. One by one, more northern provinces were controlled by the Communists. After they had essentially taken over northern China, Mao Zedong announced that his new government would soon encompass all of China.

Financial Crises

In order to keep financing his military engagements, Chiang Kai-shek simply printed more money. That inevitably led to inflation, and the value of the Chinese dollar plummeted. People saw their savings wiped out, and no help from the government was forthcoming. Price and wage controls were put into place to slow the inflation, but it was too late for that. So, Chiang Kai-shek called upon the United States, Britain, France, and the Soviet Union to help settle the differences between the Nationalists and the Communists. Because of these joint efforts, the Nationalists signed a non-aggression pact with the Communists. To help alleviate financial strains, the Soviet Union gave China credits for $250 million, and the other countries contributed $263.5 million.

The Communists again sent their list of demands to General Zhang Zhizhong, the representative of the Nationalist forces. Their demands included: 1) the punishment of "war criminals," 2) the abrogation of the constitution passed by the Nationalist-led assembly, 3) the abolition of the governments, 4) the reorganization of the army, 5) land reform, 6) the abrogation of "treasonous treaties," and 7) the creation of a national coalition without the Nationalists.

By 1949, Chiang Kai-shek and the Nationalists had lost their bid to control China. Chiang Kai-shek then resigned as the president of the Republic of China. His next in command, Li Zongren, took over. Chiang Kai-shek took $200 million in gold and US dollars from the Chinese treasury, which he said he was using to protect the Nationalist government. Li desperately needed that money to pay his troops and shore up the government, but Chiang refused to release it.

After some consternation over Li's proposed choice for a premier, Chiang finally agreed to accept the proposal proffered by Yan Xishan, a former warlord. Despite his shaky background, Yan had some finesse in diplomatic matters, and he became premier in June 1949. Li and Chiang argued about money, and Chiang expressed some of his ideas toward resolving the dispute between Mao and the Nationalists.

Yan had advised Li to move his government to Canton from Nanjing, as the Communists had tight control over the areas surrounding Nanjing. Finally, Li acquiesced and moved it. Li had difficulty organizing the Kuomintang military and gathered too many of his forces into the area around Canton rather than in other strategic areas in southern China where the Communists weren't strong. Li was hoping that the United States would send forces to help him there, but they didn't. Chiang Kai-shek decided to release some of the money he was holding from the Chinese treasury, but it wasn't enough to make a real difference. Chiang Kai-shek's constant interference made Li furious, and he started ousting strong Chiang supporters from the Kuomintang.

When the Communists suddenly conquered Canton in October 1949, Li was forced to flee to Chongqing. When he arrived, Li effectively surrendered the presidency and left for America for a medical procedure. Chiang tried to put up a defense with the forces left, but he was unsuccessful. He then was airlifted with his wife and family to Taiwan in December 1949.

After this happened, Mao Zedong announced that the new government of China was the People's Republic of China.

However, Chiang Kai-shek resumed his role as president of the Republic of China in 1950 from Taiwan. For years, he promoted a movement called Project National Glory, which was the attempt to regain mainland China from the Communists. Many Chinese émigrés who lived in Taiwan initiated various political groups, like the China Democratic Socialist Party, to support the return of the Republic of China. Chiang Kai-shek never set foot on his native soil again.

The People's Republic of China

Mao came into office and swept through the country like a cyclone. He promoted himself as a hero to the workers and the underclass. The society he envisioned was a society of the common man, speaking with one voice and thinking with one mind. He killed many of those whom he considered wealthy capitalists, as their existence and interference with affairs wouldn't create the society he dreamed of. He also encouraged workers to report on their employers if they were corrupt and distributed children's books that taught children to report on their parents, neighbors, and friends if they felt these people were criticizing Mao or the government. Thousands were arrested and were either sent to labor camps or shot.

Mao believed that intellectuals needed to understand how the common man lived, so he sent them to farms to be educated by the peasants about providing food for an entire country. This was called the Down to the Countryside Movement, which took place in the late 1960s and early 1970s. They were also required to work in factories. Having been suddenly transplanted from what they were accustomed to, they had difficulty adjusting. Suicides were common, and bodies fell from roofs in the cities. It even got to the point that pedestrians didn't walk on the sidewalks.

Sino-Soviet Split

A split occurred between Nikita Khrushchev and Mao Zedong over a period of time, but it finally culminated in 1961. The split had to do with their interpretations of communism. Mao felt that Khrushchev was too flexible in the application of communist principles. The Soviet system was "top-heavy," with numerous levels of management. Although it did lend itself to the obedience of a cult of personality, like that fostered by Mao, the Soviets had a multitude of agencies. Mao was a staunch Marxist-Leninist and believed in the succession of revolutions as leading to the creation of an ideal society under the leadership of one person and his vision. He felt that Khrushchev was too "revisionist" in his thinking and often softened or even altered his viewpoint in response to an international event or bend to persuasion by another country.

On another level, Mao objected to the intrusion of the Soviets into Chinese society, as it was too reminiscent of the vassal state structure. Mao believed that the Chinese and the Russians were two different peoples, and he believed that China had to arrange their society in such a way as to benefit the Chinese people.

A Great Leap Forward

Mao believed in a planned economy. In 1958, he created a program called the Great Leap Forward. Its aim was to transform China from an agrarian to an industrial, communist society. Grain distribution and the fruit of harvests were nationalized, requiring the growers to work in communes and huge commercialized farms. The objective was to create large amounts of food while decreasing the human labor necessary to produce it. Harvests were sent to the government for equal distribution amongst the people. Certain quotas were expected, so a family might be left with very little if their harvest was less than they'd hoped for. Because mechanization of huge farms lagged behind, farmers often couldn't meet their quotas. Food distribution efforts were unsuccessful, as there was a lack of organization, which led to grocery store shelves being half-empty. Between 1959 and 1961, there was a great famine in China, which occurred because of several factors: 1) the practice of close cropping and deep plowing reduced production, 2) as many as eighteen million youths moved to the cities by 1962, 3) Chairman Mao refused to accept international help and released incorrect data as to the depth of the crisis, and 4) the implementation of the "Four Pests Program." This program sought to eliminate pests like the Eurasian tree sparrow, which ate fruit and seeds. However, that sparrow also consumes insects. When the avian population diminished, locusts descended upon the fields and consumed the foliage, killing the crops.

Between 20 and 45 million people starved. By 1962, it was clear that the Great Leap Forward program was a dismal failure.

The Cultural Revolution

In 1966, Mao instituted the Cultural Revolution. He was convinced that anti-communist elements and capitalism were undermining the welfare of the common man or what was called the proletariat. Anti-communist elements had to be eliminated, whether they were a member of the bourgeoisie or a capitalist.

The Marxist-Leninist variety of communism advocated a class struggle in order to rid society of whatever was perceived as detrimental to the common good. As a result, capitalism was seen as the perennial enemy of the people. Mao isolated the Five Black Categories: landlords, wealthy farmers, counter-revolutionaries, bad elements of society—meaning those who didn't promote communism or Mao Zedong—and rightists.

People deemed to be in the Five Black Categories were persecuted, imprisoned, and/or executed. Universities were closed, and civil service examinations were abolished. Mao felt that education tended to produce capitalists who exploited the workers and peasants.

Mao didn't entirely subscribe to Marxism-Leninism, though. He was a megalomaniac who wanted his own brand of communism promoted. Toward promoting blind loyalty, he created a book of sayings casually called the *Little Red Book*, which were distributed to the people.

Bourgeois values were to be eschewed, as they were the antithesis of the socialist aspects of communism. Because the youth were more energetic in political endeavors, Mao encouraged them to chide their elders for promoting any bourgeois ideals. Children's books espousing his values were even distributed in food stores for youths to read, and they even recommended that children turn in their neighbors and even family members if they spoke out against the government.

Mao became very concerned that others in the government were trying to usurp him and attempted to purge his government of those people. The Communist Party President, Liu Shaoqi, became a target, and Mao dismissed him as president. Other members who were military commanders or government officials were also purged. They were labeled as "counter-revolutionaries," but Mao felt they simply stood in his way toward autocratic power and needed to find a way to push them out.

These purges were drastic. There were many massacres, and at times, due to the famine, cannibalism took place. It is impossible to know how many died during the Cultural Revolution. Estimates range from hundreds of thousands to twenty million people.

Richard Nixon Visits

After the failure of the Republic of China under Chiang Kai-shek, China went essentially silent. Because it was such a large and influential country in the East, Western countries were left to imagine how the Chinese perceived their role in international affairs. The United States and Chiang Kai-shek had often had face-to-face visits, in which each discussed their objectives and goals and created processes through which they might cooperate. But ever since Chairman Mao took office, that dialogue was non-existent.

In 1971 and 1972, US President Nixon and US Secretary of State Henry Kissinger met Mao in 1971 and 1972. These visits were very important, as the United States and the West, in general, felt that misunderstandings would inevitably develop if one party wasn't participating in discussions about issues that affected all the parties involved, like the possibility of trade.

Prior to the visit, Mao and Nixon decided their roles were not to argue ideologies but to focus on common interests. The United States was concerned about Mao's views on Korea and Vietnam. America also wanted to send a signal to the Soviet Union that issues about the region should include input from China as well. The meetings eventually led to the opening up of relations between China and the US.

Mao Zedong died in 1976 and was succeeded by Deng Xiaoping. Deng Xiaoping did not become the official leader until later, but for all intents and purposes, he ruled the country. Deng's first act was to reject Mao's Cultural Revolution. He felt that it created ignorance, fear, and chaos. He also reinstated civil service examinations and reopened the colleges.

Deng was very interested in international trade. He competed with other countries and campaigned for the export of manufactured products. It was very advantageous to the economy, and China was able to develop and produce its own goods efficiently and inexpensively.

Boluan Fanzheng

Deng wanted to reconcile with the intellectuals and elements that had been ostracized by Mao. In 1977, he proposed the idea of Boluan Fanzheng, the intent of which was to correct the unbalanced attitudes thrust upon the population by Mao. Once Deng became the paramount leader in 1978, he implemented the program.

Other Reforms

Term limits were then established, and Deng proposed that the country draft a new constitution, which was written in 1982 and is still in effect today. To reduce the confusion, he summarized China's society as based upon the Four Cardinal Principles: socialism, a dictatorship run by the people, support of the Chinese Communist Party, and adherence to the principles of Marxism-Leninism. This technique presented the people with a structure upon which they could depend. However, not everyone agreed with it.

Tiananmen Square

In 1989, students rose up in protest when they objected to some of the effects of Deng's reforms. Nepotism and corruption reigned, and students felt they didn't have equal opportunities to attain jobs. Colleges focused on teaching only social sciences, and there was little opportunity to learn about and participate in politics. That was left to the purvey of favored elites. There was no freedom of the press and speech, and there were no democratic institutions.

When Hu Yaobang, a man who was for the reform of the communist government, died, students were upset, believing that his heart attack had been triggered by the forced resignation of his position as general secretary. Small gatherings appeared in Tiananmen Square on April 15th, the day after Hu's death. Thousands appeared in the square by April 17th, and at the height of the protest, there were nearly a million demonstrators.

The government couldn't agree on what to do with the protestors, with some wanting to open up a dialogue and others wanting to get rid of the problem with brute force. On the other hand, the protestors' goals varied greatly, making the opening of a dialogue hard to do.

Deng, afraid the protests would continue to get out of hand and threaten the power of the Communist Party, declared martial law on May 20th. Tanks were sent into the square to clear it, along with armed soldiers. By June 4th, the protests were over, with thousands of people, mainly students, dead. Protests broke out around China in response to this, with some being brutally suppressed, causing even more deaths.

It is impossible to nail down a precise figure for those who died in the Tiananmen Square protests. The official number China gave was 300, but modern estimates put the number closer to 2,500 and 3,000 deaths. The world called this a massacre, and many countries cut off their arms shipments to China and imposed other embargoes.

President Xi Jinping

Elected in 2013, Xi Jinping is China's current president. He recognized the effects of nepotism and worked on eliminating that. However, his position is an autocratic one, as he eliminated the term limits placed by Deng Xiaoping during his term. Early on in his administration, Xi worked on consolidating his power. When he became president, he established a policy called Xi Jinping Thought. This ideology is meant to guide the Communist Party of China into a new and brighter future. An interesting note of this set of beliefs, which is part of China's constitution, is that it places Xi Jinping as the third leader of the People's Republic of China after Mao Zedong and Deng Xiaoping, essentially erasing Xi's two predecessors, Hu Jintao and Jiang Zemin.

For many years, China has nationalized its industries, including agriculture. However, Xi feels that its long-standing practices have produced bloated industries owned by the state and have stunted creativity and variety.

In order to promote trade, China established the One Belt One Road program. It promotes the use of the old trade routes of the past, supports upgrading them, and supports the creation of a network for the transportation of goods and products. China's economy has been slowing over the past decade, and the One Belt One Road project promises to spur the development of infrastructure.

Xi appears to be more sensitive to preventing corruption in the government and has penalized scores of government officials. In his campaign for the presidency, he promised to crack down on the "tigers and flies," which refers to both high-ranking and low-ranking leaders. Since he has taken office, over 100,000 people have been charged with corruption.

Centralization of Power

Soon after taking office, Xi created a series of Central Leading Groups. These groups are like consulting groups for society but with more authority. Among them are leading groups for cultural protection, energy resources, science and technology, environmental protection, marketing, and the stimulation of biotechnical research.

The Seven Dangers

Xi has indicated that there are seven dangers associated with Western values:

> 1. Constitutional democracy with separation of powers and judicial independence
>
> 2. Universal values contrary to Maoist principles
>
> 3. The belief that individual rights are paramount to the collective rights of the state
>
> 4. Liberal economic values and globalization
>
> 5. "Historical nihilism," meaning criticism of past errors
>
> 6. Media independence
>
> 7. Questioning of the Chinese style of socialism

In addition, Xi believes in internet censorship. Wikipedia has been blocked, along with some features of Facebook and Google. Blogging isn't forbidden, but the Chinese are warned to avoid talking about politics, controversial topics, or those that are contrary to communist principles.

Human Rights

Currently, the United Nations Human Rights Committee, Human Rights in China, Human Rights Watch, Amnesty International, and two non-governmental agencies have indicated that the current ruler of China has denied basic human rights to the citizens, such as freedom of speech and freedom of religion. Authorities in the People's Republic of China have registered objections to those assertions, however.

In addition, Xi has put ethnic Uyghurs in reeducation camps for purposes of indoctrination. In 2020, President Donald Trump signed the Uyghur Human Rights Act, imposing sanctions on officials responsible for these internments.

Republic of China

According to the Treaty of Shimonoseki of 1895, the Cairo Conference of 1943, and the defeat of Japan in 1945, the Republic of China is a political entity that is separate from the People's Republic of China. The Republic of China operates from Taiwan. Ever since it was formalized as a political entity, its status is controversial. Some say it is against international law, as the Republic of China lost its seat in the United Nations in 1971.

As mentioned above, the government of what would be the Republic of China was moved by Chiang Kai-shek in 1949. Chiang planned on moving it back to mainland China at some point but was unable to do so due to the victory of the Communists, who formed the People's Republic of China. Nonetheless, fourteen UN members still recognize it, as they want to keep all diplomatic channels open. The political status of the Republic of China is ambiguous because of the lack of a declaration of independence that is formally recognized by the international community.

The People's Republic of China believes in the One-China policy, which means that there is only one China, and since both governments have "China" in their name, only one of the governments is legitimate. There has been a push in recent years to either create the Republic of Taiwan or unite both governments.

Conclusion

China was and still is a country filled with people from many ethnic backgrounds who all nurture the guiding principle of unification. Throughout its entire history, other countries have attempted to intrude, such as the nomadic tribes from the north in its early history, Mongolia in the 13th century, Japan in the 19th and 20th centuries. Many countries have meddled in Chinese affairs, including the Russians, the British, the Portuguese, the Americans, and the peoples from the steppe regions of Asia. Pirates raided its shores from the South Pacific, and smugglers infiltrated its cities. However, in the end, the Chinese people learned to rely on themselves, although it was a very bumpy road.

After all, they weathered through a series of dynasties for centuries. China is said to have been born around 2100 BCE with the Xia dynasty, and throughout the years, the Chinese government was subject to internecine conflicts, sabotage, murder, petty jealousies, and internal corruption. The common people of the vast area of China, which is nearly four million square miles, although the area of the nation changed throughout history, had to deal with the fallout, which at times led to their deaths.

Despite this, the Chinese are people who have always told their stories, and their culture is still permeated with traditions and legends from long ago. Their tale is the story of revolution, of reaching for something better with each uprising.

Although Western audiences might not agree with the path China has taken, as their current government goes against democratic ideals, it is hard for anyone to argue the beauty of the art and writing that China has produced. Millions of people around the world imitate the beauty of Chinese silk paintings, porcelain, and poetry. Millions of people eat rice, and millions of people stir fry, deep fry, and steam their food like the Chinese did thousands of years ago. We credit the Chinese with the discovery of fireworks and gunpowder. Their history has inspired the creation of many video games and unique tales told over and over. The history of China is one that impacts all of us, and it is one that will continue to influence us for years to come.

Bibliography

Clements, J. (2010). A Brief History of Kublai Khan. Running Press.
"East Asia: Southeast Asia: China" Retrieved from
https://www.cia.gov/library/publications/the-world-
factbook/geos/ch.html
"Communist China's Painful Human Rights Story," Retrieved from
https://www.cfr.org/article/communist-chinas-painful-human-rights-
story

Guanzhong, L. & Palmer, M. (trans.) (2018 reprint). The Romance of
the Three Kingdoms. Penguin Classics.

"History of Gunpowder," Retrieved from
https://www.thoughtco.com/gunpowder-history-1991395
Hung, H. H. (2017). The Brilliant Reign of the Kangxi Emperor:
China's Qing Dynasty. Algora Publishing.
Kim, S. (2017). Ginseng and Borderland: Territorial Boundaries and
Political Relations between Qing China and Choson Korea, 1636-
1912. University of California Press, 1ˢᵗ ed.

Levy, H. "The Bifurcation of the Yellow Turbans in the Later Han,"
Retrieved from https://brill.com/view/journals/orie/13/1/article-
p251_11.xml

Man, J. (2004). Kublai Khan: The Mongol Who Remade China. Bantam Books.

Man, J. (2006). Kublai Khan. Bantam Books.

"Manchu Conquest of China," Retrieved from https://teachwar.wordpress.com/resources/war-justifications-archive/manchu-conquest-of-china-1618/

Melton, G. (2014). Faiths across Time: 5,000 Years of Religious. History ABC-CLIO.

Morgan, D. (1986). The Mongols. Blackwell Publishers.

Polo, M. (1918 reprint). The Travels of Marco Polo the Venetian. E. P. Dutton.

"Republic of China's Diplomatic Archives: Lessons of History," Retrieved from https://teachwar.wordpress.com/resources/war-justifications-archive/manchu-conquest-of-china-1618/

Sterling, C. "Visualizing Traditional China," Retrieved from https://zhang.digitalscholar.rochester.edu/china/tag/yang-guang/

Waldron, A. (1992). The Great Wall of China: From History to Myth. Cambridge University Press.

Werner, E.T.C. (2005), Retrieved from https://www.gutenberg.org/files/15250/15250-h/15250-h.htm#d0e1278

Wriggins, S. (2003 rev.). The Silk Road Journey with Xuanzang. Westview Press.

Wuyong, Q. & Novel, B. (trans.) (2019). Fortune-teller Next to the Beauty: Vol 18. Funstory.

"Zhu Qizhen: The Zhengtong Emperor," Retrieved from https://www.mingtombs.eu/emp/06zhengtong/zhengtong.html

Here's another book by Captivating History
that you might be interested in

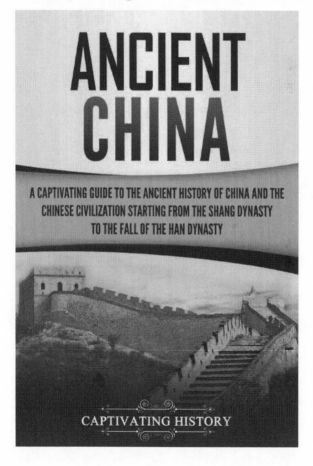

Made in the USA
Middletown, DE
11 March 2024

51195887R00071